Creative
KITCHEN
Decorating

First published in the United Kingdom in 1996 by Hamlyn
an imprint of Reed International Books Ltd
Michelin House, 81 Fulham Road, London, SW3 6RB
and Auckland, Melbourne, Singapore and Toronto

ISBN 0 600 58999 4

Cover design by Senate

Cover photographs:
Front Cover Blue and white diagonal tiles – Fired Earth; Steel coffee pot and
grinder – Chippendale Kitchens; Wooden herb container – David Barrett/Homes
and Gardens/Robert Harding; Bowl with eggs and container with wooden
spoons – Graham Rae/Eaglemoss; *Front Flap* Blue cockerel plate and napkin –
Simon Page-Ritchie/Eaglemoss; *Back Cover* Shaker utensil holder – John
Suett/Eaglemoss; Latticed kitchen window – Elizabeth Whiting Associates;
Modern kitchen with steel units – Worldwide Syndication Ltd

Printed and bound in Hong Kong

HAMLYN

Guide to Creating Your Home

Creative KITCHEN Decorating

HAMLYN

CONTENTS

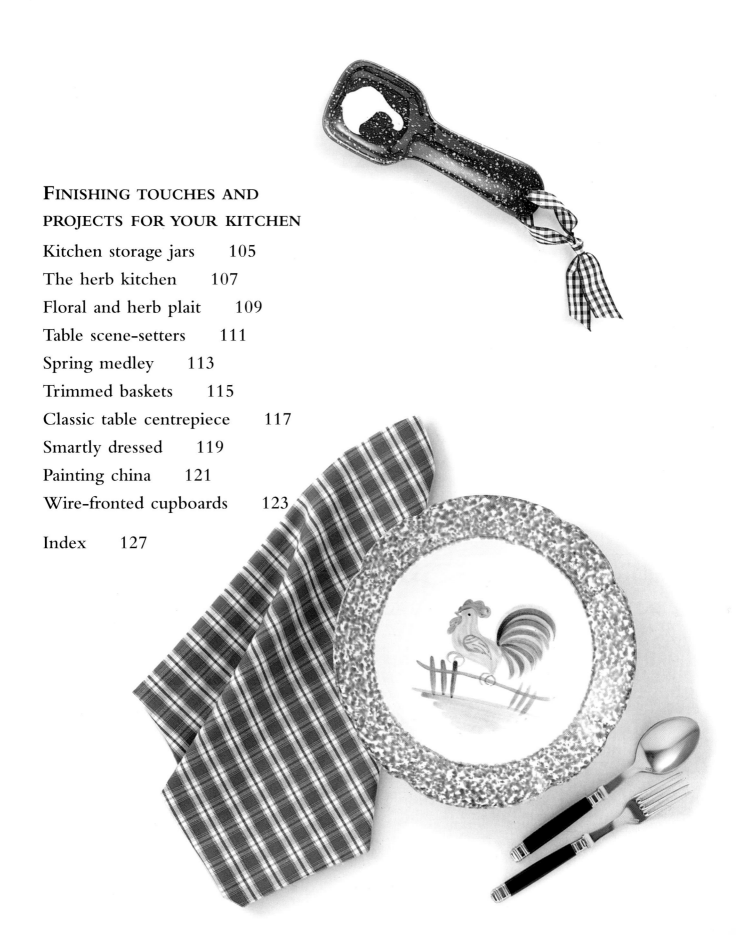

FINISHING TOUCHES AND PROJECTS FOR YOUR KITCHEN

ALL ABOUT KITCHENS

The traditional heart of a house, a successful kitchen is efficient, attractive and comfortable – a place where you can enjoy working and relaxing.

The efficiency of a kitchen depends more on how it's laid out than how spacious it is. Though many people long for a big kitchen, a well planned small one has plenty of potential.

It is important to consider your lifestyle when planning your kitchen. Do you eat in your kitchen? If so, how often does the family eat together? Is there more than one cook? Do you like to entertain in the kitchen? If you've got enough space, it may be better to have a small kitchen and separate dining area or one large area combining both.

A well planned kitchen, like this double galley style, is both efficient and pleasant to work in.

THE WORK PATH

When you are planning your kitchen, always aim to make the relationship between the food storage, preparation, cooking and serving areas as practical and energy-saving as possible.

Cooking a meal usually follows a predictable pattern involving particular areas of activity: food storage (fridge and food cupboards); preparation (worktops and sink); and cooking (oven and hob or cooker top).

Although you may often have to double back on yourself, the most sensible layout is based on a work path of fridge/worktop/sink/worktop/cooker/worktop.

This logical sequence means the cook will have the minimum of legwork. Though the dimensions vary depending on the available size and shape, the basic principle can be applied to every kitchen. (See the area shaded grey on the kitchen plans of different layouts.)

Ideally, the total length of the sides of your work path should be 4-7 metres (3½-6½ yards). Distances any greater create needless kitchen mileage; any smaller will leave you feeling cramped.

Parts of the house, such as doors and windows, also determine how the space can be used, and take into account the position of electric sockets and plumbing.

THE CLASSIC LAYOUTS

A kitchen can be almost any shape or size, depending on the architecture of the building. But there are six basic layouts which, within the guidelines of the work path, will give you a practical kitchen.

Most kitchens are based on a double galley, U or L shape, and some have the addition of a central island unit or a peninsula arm. The smallest type of kitchen is likely to be the single line.

THE SINGLE LINE

Where the kitchen must be fitted into a very narrow space, often the only possible layout is the single line where the units and appliances are all installed along one wall. This can look very efficient and streamlined. Place the sink in the middle and choose built-under appliances so you can make the most of all the available worktop space. Ideally, the room should be at least wide enough for two people to pass each other; a worktop with a cut-away bay may be a sensible option for a very narrow kitchen.

Some single line kitchens can be spacious – when the units and appliances are ranged along one wall of a family room or combined kitchen-diner, for example – but usually space is at a premium in a single line layout. The kitchen is often a corridor and through traffic can be a distraction. Plan with safety in mind, and keep cooking areas away from the doors into and out of the kitchen.

In a small kitchen it's unlikely there will be space for a table or breakfast bar, but you may be able to fit in a pull-out or pull-down flap and folding chairs for informal meals for one or two.

THE L LINE

With this versatile layout the units and appliances are arranged on two adjacent walls, creating an efficient path of work protected from through traffic. Make sure that the corner is used to best effect – a carousel in the corner cupboard is often a good solution. Separate the sink, cooking area and fridge with stretches of worktop to avoid the areas of greatest activity becoming too congested.

If this sort of layout is part of a larger area, perhaps a dining room, it makes sense to site the work path well away from other activities in the room.

THE U SHAPE

One of the most adaptable of all layouts, the U shape has three walls for units and appliances. A small U shape kitchen is like a double galley with the advantage of a third wall. As the kitchen is uninterrupted by through traffic, it forms an efficient and safe arrangement in a compact area.

Scale is important: you need enough space between facing units for two people to work without bumping into each other, while too large a space leads to unnecessary walking about.

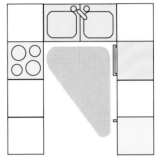

THE DOUBLE GALLEY

Similar to the single line but usually wider, the double galley has the advantage of units lined along facing walls. The linking wall often can't be used because of a door or window, but an efficient work path is generally possible. Ideally, the room should be at least 2.4m (8ft) wide if there's a door at either end and there is frequent through traffic; consider one or two cut-away worktop bays if passing space is tight.

The double galley is usually a compact and efficient layout for one or two people to work in, but for access to low cupboards make sure there's at least 1.2m (4ft) between facing units.

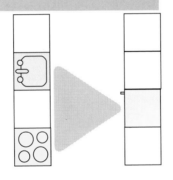

THE PENINSULA

In a larger room or kitchen/dining room, the peninsula is a flexible layout. The short arm jutting out into the room usually divides the cooking and eating areas. The arm can house a sink or cooking rings, if necessary with an

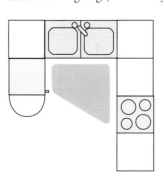

extractor hood above, or it can do double duty as an extra working surface and a breakfast bar or serving area.

Essentially, the island layout is a larger version of the L or U shape, with an additional work area in the middle. It can look stunning, but is practical only in a spacious room. Careful planning is needed to avoid wasteful journeys around the island.

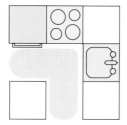

COMPUTER PLANNING

Though the final decisions on the planning and style of your kitchen are yours, kitchen planning services and computer aided designs have taken a lot of the hard work out of planning a workmanlike kitchen. Offered by many manufacturers, these planning services allow you to view a whole range of options in a short space of time.

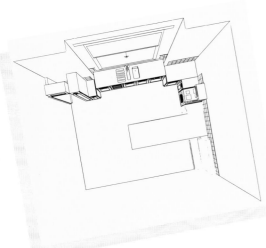

Computer print-outs of designs based on the precise shape and size of your kitchen allow you to view a particular layout from various angles. From these, you can choose an attractive layout based on an efficient work path.

After your kitchen has been surveyed to assess any technical problems, you can watch the design taking shape on screen.

LIGHTING A KITCHEN

Well planned lighting is an essential ingredient of a successful and workable kitchen. It helps you to perform tasks safely and efficiently, and transforms a functional area into a room you can truly enjoy.

I f you have spent time, money and effort fitting, equipping and decorating your kitchen you want to make the most of the investment, so it's vital to consider lighting from the outset. Kitchens are primarily working places, and you must plan the lighting to make food preparation and cooking as simple as possible. As in any living space, you need background light for general illumination, but in the kitchen task lighting for working areas assumes special importance. If you eat as well as cook in the kitchen, you also need to provide more atmospheric light to dine by. To come

up with the lighting scheme that is right for you, you must assess your own individual needs and working patterns.

The best kitchen lighting is not necessarily the brightest. Very bright light bouncing off glossy surfaces, such as laminate worktops, tiles or polished steel appliances, can cause a tiring glare. Keep levels of illumination fairly even to avoid an uncomfortable contrast between light and shade. In general, light sources should be positioned in front of you, and shielded so the light falls on the work surface and does not shine straight into your eyes.

Hi-tech recessed spotlights illuminate the work area in this modern kitchen, with lights mounted in the cooker hood. Unusual aluminium pendent lights illuminate the kitchen table and contribute to the overall style of the room.

GENERAL LIGHTING

The purpose of general lighting in a kitchen is to provide safe and relatively even levels of illumination without undermining the character of the room. In a small kitchen, a ceiling-mounted fixture which emits light in all directions, such as a glass globe, may be sufficient. In most situations, however, a single source is not enough. A pendent fitting, on its own, casts shadows on to the worktop, so you are literally standing in your own light.

The best strategy is to provide a number of different light sources which you can angle to wash the walls or the ceiling with light, creating a general background glow rather than a single bright focus. Track lighting mounted on the ceiling is flexible and adjustable. Individual spotlights do the same job, but installing a number of spotlights entails more disruption to finishes than putting up a single track. Ceiling-mounted downlighters are very unobtrusive – choose the eyeball variety for maximum flexibility.

Wall lights come in a variety of styles and are a good solution if you have enough free wall space. Concealed lights fixed to the top of wall units bounce light off the ceiling. You can fit general lighting to a dimmer switch to allow you to adjust the light level.

TASK LIGHTING

Poorly lit kitchens are hazardous places. Chopping and slicing with sharp knives, cooking with open pots and pans, and using ovens and other appliances pose risks which are magnified if you can't see what you're doing clearly. Safety is not the only consideration. Cooking involves making all kinds of visual judgements, which demand shadow- and glare-free working conditions.

A simple, efficient way to light a worktop is to fit strip lighting under a run of wall units. This is standard in the design of many fitted units. Shield the light source with a baffle or decor strip and make sure it's hidden from sitting as well as standing positions. Fit the light towards the front to light the entire work surface evenly.

If you don't have wall units directly over your worktop, you can install wall lights, or recessed or surface-mounted lights on the ceiling above. Remember to light the sink area as well as the cooking and preparation areas. Many cooker hoods incorporate a light to illuminate the rings. It's also useful to fit lights in larders or deep storage cupboards – these can be triggered by opening the door.

TYPES OF LIGHT SOURCE

The three principal sources of artificial light are fluorescent, tungsten and low-voltage halogen bulbs. Each has its advantages and disadvantages for kitchen use.

❖ Fluorescent tubes are economical and long-lasting, but they give a cold light unless special tubes are used.
❖ Tungsten, the ordinary domestic light source, is warmer in appearance but the bulbs need frequent replacement.
❖ Low-voltage halogen bulbs are increasingly favoured for kitchens: they are small and unobtrusive and the quality of light is clear and faithful to true colours. Dichromic halogen lights have the sparkle and clarity of standard halogen but are cooler. Both need a transformer to convert the mains voltage.

▣ *Halogen eyeball spotlights sparkle in the ceiling of this streamlined kitchen and create a good level of general light. You can angle them as required, to ensure the work surfaces are well lit.*

▲ *The clean lines of this white kitchen are enhanced with clever lighting mounted under the wall units and hidden by plain decor strips.*

◀ *The cooker fits neatly into the fireplace opening in this traditional kitchen – strip lighting hidden behind the wooden surround shines on to the white tiles, making the area a focal point. A rise-and-fall pendent light, positioned in front of the window, lights the work area, preventing shadows from being cast.*

◀ *Strip lighting mounted under the wall units efficiently illuminates the worktop with pools of light. During the daytime the sink area benefits from natural light.*

EATING AREAS

Sitting down to enjoy a meal calls for atmospheric lighting. In kitchen/dining rooms which fall neatly into two distinct areas, you can arrange the lighting in the eating part of the room to provide a warmer, more hospitable mood. Wall lights such as sconces or uplights on dimmer switches make soft background illumination, with a pendant over the dining table for more local, intimate light. You can adjust rise-and-fall pendants to the right glare-free height; otherwise, fit silvered bulbs to prevent light from shining straight into your eyes.

Eating areas which are directly incorporated within the main kitchen pose a greater challenge. You can install a pendant or downlighters over the table and fit general lighting to a dimmer switch so that the kitchen fades into the background while you are eating your meal.

Adjustable spotlights illuminate the working area of the kitchen, while a rise-and-fall pendent light hung low over the table lights the dining area. The shade on the pendant ensures the light is glare free.

◧ *A simple but elegant row of pendent lights fitted with glass decor bulbs illuminates the breakfast bar in this kitchen, giving each place setting its own intimate pool of light.*

◨ *A dramatic pendent fitting over the table ensures adequate lighting while reinforcing the hi-tech aspects of this kitchen. Glass-fronted cupboards are fitted with built-in lights to illuminate the worktop, and are also lit from inside to display favourite glassware and china.*

KITCHEN STORAGE

If space in your kitchen is limited, think about improving and reorganizing existing storage space and adding some simple new storage ideas. You'll be amazed at the difference it makes.

L ack of storage space in your kitchen can make life extremely frustrating. Over-filled cupboards and drawers make it virtually impossible to find anything, crowded worktops mean that there isn't enough room for preparing food, and keeping the kitchen tidy and surfaces clean is a nightmare. In addition to this, wall units stacked to capacity are dangerous, as heavy cans and crockery may fall and injure someone or smash on to the floor.

Finding more storage space doesn't necessarily mean making major structural alterations or fitting a new kitchen. There are under-used areas in most kitchens, which you can adapt to provide additional storage. Being well organized helps too – you can fit more into a tidy cupboard than a cluttered one.

Before you change anything in your existing scheme, consider the following. Does everything currently in your kitchen need to be there? Think about alternative sites for appliances such as the freezer, washing machine and tumble dryer. Putting them in a garage can free extra space for an additional base unit or a set of shelves. Under the stairs or in a cellar is another possible site. But check that it is possible to extend the water supply and drainage for laundry equipment before making the move. If moving laundry equipment proves impossible, stacking the tumble dryer on top of the washing machine frees space for other uses.

There are many ways to increase storage space in a cramped kitchen. Here, shelves built across a window and over the cooker create two more surfaces. A metal rail behind the hob (cooking rings) solves the problem of storing awkwardly shaped utensils.

FINDING MORE SPACE

It's also a good idea to work out what sort of additional storage space you really need. For instance, if your worktops are constantly covered with gadgets, utensils and storage jars, then you need accessible storage which frees this area but still leaves frequently used items close to hand. If finding space for the weekly shopping is always a problem, then your priority is more storage space for food.

FOOD STORAGE

Is your fridge big enough to cope with all your grocery needs? A tall fridge takes up no more floor space than a shorter model. If you invest in one which offers zoned cooling, ranging from 1-7°C (34-45°F), you are able to store everything from cook-chill dishes to salads in the safest condition.

How much space do you need for dry goods and canned foods? Even if you can't add any more cupboard space, you can make the most of what you've already got. Invest in a selection of tiered shelf stackers. These allow you to store food on three levels, so it's easy to see immediately what's in the cupboard. You can bring the back of a cupboard door into action as a space-saver, too. Providing the door still shuts against any existing shelves, you can fit a set of narrow wire shelves on the inside to provide easily accessible space for jars of spices, herbs and other frequently used small items.

Narrow shelves or specially made midway units fitted between the wall and base units make another handy place to store slim jars and bottles.

◪ *Stainless steel wall-hung racks for spices, utensils and kitchen paper leave the surfaces tidy and reflect the hi-tech theme of the kitchen. Wire shelves fit neatly above the cooker hood and extra wall shelving allows condiments, sauces and seasonings to be displayed within easy reach for cooking.*

◪ *Food and utensils are stored out of the way on this space-saving rack. Suspended from the ceiling it provides handy hanging space for pots, pans and utensils and supports a glass shelf for storage jars.*

◩ *An under-shelf basket that clips on to the shelf above makes practical use of otherwise under-utilized space between the shelves in a kitchen unit.*

◪ *A two-tier carousel fits into an existing corner unit to give you easy access to the deepest reaches of a corner cupboard.*

▼ *No space is wasted in this kitchen. A useful wall rack has been fixed on to the small area behind the sink. A plate rack makes use of an equally small area of wall between the window and door. Cups and jugs hang from hooks along the top and bottom of the rack.*

EQUIPMENT

If your cutlery drawer is filled to bursting, you can ease the congestion with a two-tier cutlery tray. Remove any large objects, such as draining spoons and fish slices and store them near the cooker in an attractive container, or hanging from a wall rack.

Alternatively hang them from a wall- or ceiling-mounted storage rack. A traditional wooden clothes airer suspended from the ceiling is an inexpensive way to add hanging storage. You can hang pans and utensils using S-shaped butchers' hooks, and put eggs, lemons, garlic and small utensils such as icing nozzles and mini cake tins in hanging wire baskets.

You can also fit a metal or wooden wall grid, or a simple rail between the base and wall units. Custom-made rail systems are available with clip-on wire baskets, cookery book holders, knife racks and other useful accessories.

Alternatively, you can make your own wall hanger, by attaching two large eyelet fittings to the wall; use a painted broom handle, or length of copper or chrome piping to provide

the rail. Using a length of curtain pole is another option – the new metal types, with ends shaped into arrowheads or shepherds' crooks are attractive in most kitchen settings.

Wicker or terracotta wall baskets, sold for holding plants, are another possibility for storing a variety of utensils, small packets and jars.

Fitting a carousel into corner base units makes good sense, since it gives you access to most of the area inside the cupboard. Don't store pans in base units unless you have to, as they take up a lot of room. Buy a floor-standing tiered pan rack instead.

The space between the floor and the bottom of base units – hidden by a clip-on plinth – is often a forgotten area which can provide invaluable space for flat pieces of baking equipment such as trays and flan rings or spare plates, larger serving platters and other things you need to keep but don't use every day. You can ask a carpenter to replace the plinth with a series of narrow pullout drawers made to match the units.

17

SIMPLE STORAGE SOLUTIONS

❖ Use open shelves where a lack of space makes fitting a cupboard either awkward or impossible. Attach hooks to the edge or underneath of the shelves for hanging jugs, cups and mugs from their handles.

❖ Do away with towering and precarious stacks of plates and bowls by investing in a plate stacker. Designed along the same lines as a tiered pan rack, it copes with plates and bowls of differing sizes.

❖ Store equipment as well as vegetables in a stacking plastic or wire vegetable rack.

❖ If you are short of preparation space, look out for a wheeled, wooden trolley that has basket storage below its work surface.

❖ Fit a narrow rack, a hanging grid or hooks to the back of a kitchen door.

❖ A wall-mounted, magnetic knife strip keeps knives close at hand and out of the reach of small children.

❖ If there is space between the top of wall units and the ceiling, use it for items such as the Christmas roasting tin or preserving pans that are rarely used.

❖ Full-depth wall units are a hazard above the sink – but you can fit narrow open shelving, just wide enough to hold glass storage jars. Make even more of the space with clip-on, under-shelf baskets.

❖ Visible storage should look attractive. Decant dried foods, grains and similar items into cheap, but effective, Spanish glass jars. Keep oils and vinegars on view if you transfer them to pretty glass bottles – freeing up cupboard space. Save large food jars – after washing they make perfect storage containers.

❖ Fit glass shelves across the kitchen window. for pots of fresh herbs, glasses or small bottles.

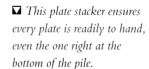
Simply screw this wire shelving rack into place on the inside of a door or on to a wall. Make sure that internal shelves, or their contents, don't get in the way when the door is closed.

This plate stacker ensures every plate is readily to hand, even the one right at the bottom of the pile.

Attractive wooden cubbyholes provide storage and display space for food jars. Utensils hang underneath on a matching green pole and S-hooks.

Here a whole wall of open shelving, both above and below the worktop level, gives a narrow kitchen much needed storage space.

KITCHEN WORK SURFACES

The worktop is the hardest working area in your kitchen, so it makes sense to choose a material tough enough to cope and surfaces tailor-made for your needs.

K itchen worktops lead a hard life. Whatever the surface you choose, it must look good and be able to shrug off stains. A worktop must also be robust enough to cope with the impact of a meal being prepared and be impervious to the thermal shock of a pan of hot food.

A continuous run of worktops provides you with ample working space, and is easy to clean as there are no gaps or crevices to trap food scraps and spilt liquid. The worktop can also double as an eating area, and as

a shelf for your food processor, electric toaster, kettle and other equipment which is used every day.

When spending time and money choosing work surfaces for your kitchen, you want to be sure they will last and look as good in years to come as when they were fitted. Think carefully before you choose your worktop – and remember your choice need not be limited to just one material. Mixing materials to suit your needs is a practical approach worth considering.

More good looking, durable materials are available for kitchen worktops now than ever before. The sleek grey worktop in this kitchen is a matt laminate, which provides a hard wearing surface for both preparation and eating areas at an affordable price.

BUYING WORKTOPS

❖ Can I fit the worktop myself?
This is not recommended unless you are very good at DIY. Laminate tops must be securely jointed to prevent moisture entering the chipboard. Cutting either laminate or solid wood for the sink and hob (cooking rings) can be difficult unless you have the right sort of electric jigsaw blade. Artificial stone and steel can only be fitted by specialists. Tiling is reasonably easy if you are applying tiles on top of an existing laminate or other suitable top, but new tiled tops are best installed by experts.

❖ How much worktop will I need?
The supplier will work this out for you. Measure the length of the walls where the worktop will be used before you go to the shop. If you are fitting a new worktop over old kitchen units, measure their depth. Modern kitchen units are a standard size, but old ones may be smaller or slightly larger.

❖ Will the colour match my kitchen units?
Make sure that you look at a worktop sample together with your kitchen units and the general decor before making a final decision. If the units are already in place, take a sample of the worktop home. If you are looking at samples in a shop, view them in both artificial light and daylight to be sure of choosing the right colour.

❖ Should I choose light or dark worktops?
The colour of the worktop should depend not just on your kitchen units and decor, but also on the amount of light the kitchen gets. Dark coloured surfaces will show spills and stains less than paler ones, but may make a dark kitchen dreary.

❖ Can I use a mixture of materials?
If you would like to use an expensive material such as artificial stone, solid wood or stainless steel but your budget won't stretch to it, think about using just a section in a main work area, such as near the hob or sink.

MATERIALS

Kitchen worktops come in a range of materials, all with different qualities. To choose the right one for your kitchen it helps to be familiar with the different types.

SOLID WOOD
Solid wood tops are made from cherry, maple, American white oak and a variety of other hardwoods, and are supplied cut to measure. They look particularly attractive with rustic style units, but they are expensive. Wood strip tops are also available. Wooden work surfaces are hard wearing, attractive and very easy to care for. Depending on the finish, accidental scratches or burns can sometimes simply be sanded away, and an occasional wipe with cooking oil is all that may be needed to keep the wood in good condition. Take advice if your kitchen is prone to dampness, as the tops may warp.

❏ *Wonderful wood*
A wooden worktop looks especially good in a traditional-style kitchen, where it adds a feeling of warmth to the surroundings.

20

LAMINATE

This is the most popular and widely available material. Laminate is made from sheets of paper soaked in chemicals then pressed and baked. The top sheet is usually printed with a pattern. It comes in many different colours and designs, including realistic granite and marble effects. The basic product is a thin, hard sheet which is glued to block or chipboard to make worktops. The finished worktops are available in either matt or glossy finishes.

Post-formed laminate worktops have a rounded front edge, while *double post-formed* tops have a rounded front edge and a small, rounded upstand at the back to fit against the wall. *Edged* worktops are also available, which have a front edge of either wood, to match the kitchen units, or ABS plastic (a dense, very hard wearing material).

Laminate worktops are easy to clean, but are subject to wear and tear. They can be scratched easily, so you must use a chopping board for cutting – a glossy laminated surface is particularly prone to scratching. A laminate surface may blister if you put a very hot pan down on it.

This type of work surface must be properly fitted, as the chipboard underneath will swell and the worktop buckle if water gets into the joints.

◢ Bright white laminate
Still the most popular choice for kitchen worktops, a huge variety of plastic laminates is available to coordinate with kitchen units. Whether sparkling white, as in this kitchen, or coloured and patterned to suit your particular scheme, there is no shortage of options.

ARTIFICIAL STONE

Artificial stone looks just like the real thing, but is made from a mixture of minerals and polymers baked to a hard scratch, stain and heat resistant finish. The material can be joined seamlessly, and may be moulded into sinks which are then an integral part of the worktop. Available in pastel colours as well as stone effects, these work surfaces have a sleek stylish look and work well with both modern and traditional units. Artificial stone worktops can be installed only by a professional fitter.

STONE

Real granite and slate can be used for worktops. The stone is available only from specialist suppliers and is cut to measure and polished before installation. Worktops are usually supplied with a rounded front edge. You can also buy thinner sheets to use as an alternative to tiling between the worktop and the wall units. Both slate and granite are heat, impact, stain and scratch resistant, but are expensive and heavy. Base units may need to be reinforced to take the weight.

If you choose stone, you will have to opt for an under-built sink, set about 3mm (⅛in) below the surface of the worktop. Grooves can then be cut into the stone at either side of the sink for draining.

◤ Artificial stone
At the luxury end of the market, a worktop made from artificial stone will go on looking good for years. With its scratch, stain and heat resistant qualities, this is one of the toughest of worktop materials.

◀ Granite style
Robust, heat resistant and easy to keep clean, this granite worktop adds real style to the kitchen. Granite is an expensive worktop material, but will continue to provide sterling service for years after installation.

TILES

Tiles used for worktops must be of worktop quality, tough enough to withstand the thermal shock of a hot pan or the impact of a dropped utensil. Ordinary wall tiles are not suitable.

Tiles are fixed to chipboard to make worktops, which can have rounded edges, or can be edged with wood to match the units.

This type of work surface looks very attractive, especially if you coordinate wall and worktop tiling, but it has its disadvantages. A tiled worktop is very difficult to clean, as food stains discolour the grouting, and because it is not a perfectly smooth surface it is unsuitable for rolling pastry or chopping food. To solve this problem, inset or use a separate hardwood, marble, granite or slate chopping block for all your food preparation.

▶ Top tiles

Worktop tiles are designed to withstand a degree of heat and impact, but they don't compromise on looks to do it. Choosing three shades of a colour for the tiles breaks up the surface nicely.

STAINLESS STEEL

Stainless steel worktops are the professional cook's choice, though some manufacturers produce them for the ordinary domestic kitchen.

Though it's not the most quiet of materials in use, steel is hard wearing and easy to clean — follow the manufacturer's care instructions for cleaning to avoid scratching the surface.

Worktops are supplied custom made, and can have hobs (cooking rings) and sinks welded in to give a sleek, seamless finish. Accessories, such as wall hanging grids for utensils and matching steel fronted appliances, will give your kitchen a high-tech and stylishly professional look.

◀ Streamlined steel

Stainless steel worktops give a streamlined, high-tech look to a kitchen, particularly if they are teamed with stainless steel utensils and accessories. Because it is so durable and is easy to keep clean, this tough, hygienic material is often favoured by professional cooks.

WORKTOP CARE

❖ Clean laminate worktops with a non-scratch liquid cleaner. Stubborn stains, such as tea, coffee or wine, can be removed with dilute bleach.

❖ Tiled worktops need frequent wiping to keep the grout in good condition. Use one of the specialist tile cleaners, or wipe over with dilute bleach.

❖ Putting a very hot pan straight on to a laminate work surface can cause blistering – and there's no cure. Keep a metal trivet beside oven and cooker top to rest pans on.

❖ Scratches or accidental burns on wooden worktops can be sanded away using fine sandpaper. Wipe over with a little cooking oil after sanding. A sparing monthly application of cooking oil all over the tops will keep the wood in good condition.

❖ Artificial stone tops are resistant to impact, scratches and heat, but can be slightly damaged by a very hot pan. If this happens, rub the burn away with fine grade sandpaper.

❖ Odourless bacteria killing cleaner – available from most supermarkets – keeps worktops free from most bacteria which can cause food poisoning.

◤ *Mixed materials*
There is no reason to keep to just one surface material in your kitchen. Here, a heat resistant marble inset covers the most hard working area around the cooker.

◣ *Contrast worktops*
For a dramatic look choose work surfaces in a contrasting colour to the rest of the kitchen. A worktop with a two-tone speckled colourway will show fewer marks and stains than a light single colour.

FINISHES FOR KITCHEN UNITS

The finish of your kitchen units determines the look of your kitchen just as much as its layout and design. Have a good look at all the materials and styles before making up your mind.

Whether you are installing a new kitchen from scratch or updating an existing one with new unit doors and drawer fronts, you're bound to have an idea of the look you want. Browsing through catalogues and visiting showrooms should give you a clearer impression of the styles you like, as well as their availability and cost.

Most manufacturers produce a range of doors and drawer fronts at different prices to fit a single set of standard kitchen units – usually 1000mm (39in), 600mm (24in) and 300mm (12in) wide. So it is often the colour and style of the unit doors that dictates the style for the whole room. In fact, replacing the doors and drawer fronts is one of the easiest ways to revamp an existing kitchen. A whole separate business has developed with companies offering made-to-measure replacement doors.

Door and matching drawer fronts exist in literally hundreds of various styles and materials. You can choose from the many woods, veneers

or mock wood finishes. Alternatively, you can opt for a laminate or high gloss laminate in one of the many different colours and finishes available. There is also a huge range of door shapes to look at, from a simple flush door to panelled styles and even more intricate details. If you decide on wooden doors you also have the choice of various different paint effects that you can buy ready-made or apply yourself.

But there is more to your choice than just the look. If you do a lot of heavy duty cooking or have a home full of teenagers, you need a hard-wearing material that won't show wear and tear easily, while in a home with small children a kitchen that can't cope with messy fingerprints is difficult to keep clean.

Ending up with a kitchen that looks good and lasts well means choosing the right finish for your door and drawer fronts. The following pages provide an introduction to the wide variety of materials on the market today.

The appearance of the unit doors and drawers makes all the difference to the image of a kitchen. Here, solid beech doors in a simple modern style are set off by plain black bar style handles. For a streamlined finish, the kitchen appliances, such as the fridge, are cleverly concealed behind door fronts too.

WOOD

Each type of wood has a typical grain and colour. The following list of the main kinds of wood used to make kitchen door and drawer fronts should help you reach a decision. The types not illustrated as units are shown as samples on the left.

LIGHT WOOD

The subtle clean colours of pale wood are ideal for a modern-looking kitchen. They range from white woods like ash to those with warmer tones of pink, rich reddish gold or light brown in cherry or mahogany.

Ash (2) is naturally pale and creamy in colour and particularly suited to plain styles of door. Its close, tight grain makes it especially resilient. Sometimes it is stained black for a thoroughly modern finish.

Birch is very hardwearing, but can shrink and distort if not carefully seasoned. It is best suited to larger kitchens where condensation is less likely to accumulate. Birch door and drawer fronts are usually quite plain.

Maple often has a pinkish hue. It is excellent for simple panelled doors that are suited to both town and country-style kitchens. It does not dent easily.

Oak is a pale, grainy timber that looks great when stained or limed. Oak door and drawer fronts often feature shaping and curved panels which are ideal for a cottage look. It is also a very durable wood.

Pine (1) is popular in both its natural state and when coloured for country style kitchens. The wood is often knotty and soft, so it dents easily when knocked.

◀ *Updated maple*
Maple suits both contemporary and traditional kitchens. The straight lines of the units in this modern version show the wood off to perfection.

▲ *Staining alder*
These alder units are finished with a lacquered cherry stain to give them a desirable warm red colour.

VENEERS

Veneer fronts are excellent value for money, combining the beauty of timber with the stability and strength of an MDF panel underneath. Many veneer door and drawer fronts are tougher than their solid wood counterparts and retain their shape well.

Veneer is often used for the interior panel of a door, where the door frame is solid wood. In this type of kitchen, check to make sure all the veneered panels colour match each other exactly.

DARKER WOODS

Dark wood kitchens are often designed in classical, elegant styles. Dark wood works well with a contrast. Chestnut or stained oak units look good teamed with light tiles or a pale worktop.

Alder is a resilient wood that is deep gold in colour. It suits plainer styles of door in modern town-style kitchens.

Beech is a close-grained wood, often with a slightly pink tone to the timber. It is widely used for the fronts of kitchen units, especially for plain, modern styles with simple panels.

Cherry (4) is a reasonably tough reddy-brown wood, but is damaged by condensation if poorly seasoned. It is used for both plain and more ornate styles of door front.

Chestnut (3) is a strong, golden-red wood well suited to kitchen units. It tends to be popular for the more ornate country style.

Mahogany (5) ranges in colour from red to dark brown. It is very rarely used nowadays because it is an endangered species. Other tropical woods such as lauan, sapele and acacia are sometimes used in place of mahogany

▷ Hardwood style

Elaborately carved solid acacia doors and drawers do much to create the warmth of a traditional kitchen.

▲ Heart of oak

Warm oak tones are ideal for a larger kitchen. The symmetrical panelling on the doors carries the eye along the run of units lining the walls.

▲ Going for a veneer

A veneered finish is a perfectly acceptable alternative to solid wood. This birch veneer has all the style of more expensive wooden units.

LAMINATES AND SIMILAR OPTIONS

A laminate is a manmade veneer that is bonded firmly to a base of board or inexpensive timber. The range of colours, surface finishes and textures of laminates is enormous. As well as timber effects and plain colours there are marbled, granite, metallic, random-coloured and high-gloss laminates which all add a really distinctive look to a room, while providing a durable surface. Some of the reproduction woods, for example, offer you a tougher finish than the natural timber.

High pressure laminate (HPL) is a true, hardwearing laminate made from layers of resin impregnated papers with a decorative surface paper on top. These are heated under extreme pressure to form a really tough surface, then applied to a door made of either high-density chipboard or MDF. The quality of HPL varies, but in general you get what you pay for.

Melamine is a single, resin-impregnated top sheet applied directly to the MDF door. Its quality is not nearly as high as HPL, but this is reflected in the price.

True laminates fit round curved or postformed edges, giving a really smooth finish to a door. The edges of melamine doors are often finished with matching edging strips. Both methods finish doors to a decent standard.

There is another method for finishing edges called foil wrapping, where only a thin top paper is wrapped over the edges. Although flexible enough to adhere to curves, this finish is not nearly as hardwearing as HPL or melamine. The foil strips are unlikely to colour match the rest of the door exactly. Whichever type of laminate you choose, make sure that the inside of the door is finished in the same material to prevent the door from warping.

High-gloss laminates High-gloss door and drawer fronts are the ultimate in modern kitchen glamour. The shiny surfaces are created in two

ways, one of which applies a lacquered coating over the backing and the other a true high-sheen laminate.

❖ Applying a lacquer of polyester to a plain MDF door in a totally dust free environment is the expensive option. Unfortunately, it shows every fingermark, chip or scratch once installed, so it's not ideal for a family kitchen.

❖ The second type of high-gloss door is the most expensive type of laminate, made by pressing the layers of paper against a highly polished surface to

◸ *An alternative to wood*
These units may look like wood, but they're not. The subtle grain and colour of the maple effect is really a hardwearing laminate.

make it extra smooth, in the same way as timber-effect laminates are pressed against a surface with a fake wood grain. They are less expensive and harder wearing than polyester lacquer, although scratches do inevitably show.

◸ *Metallic laminate*
With its mirror gloss, metallic finish in dark grey, these laminated unit fronts are perfect for an ultra-modern looking kitchen.

◪ *A timber trim*

White melamine door fronts are jazzed up with beech-patterned trims and handles. Trims like these are an economical way to introduce the warmth of natural timber.

◪ *Daring red*

High-gloss laminates give a kitchen a really glamorous look. Picking a bright colour like this scarlet-red guarantees a highly distinctive image as well.

◪ *Loving lilac*

The matt-textured laminate units in pale lilac-grey make a personal style statement in this kitchen.

MATCHING APPLIANCES

Camouflaging your kitchen appliances behind kitchen doors is an appealing idea, but you may need to replace all your appliances with special integrated versions to do so. A true integrated appliance is designed to allow for the thickness of a unit door so that, once it is in place, the front is flush with the other kitchen units.

As an alternative to this, some freestanding appliances allow you to replace their front panel – usually laminate – with one which matches the rest of the door or drawer fronts. This is often the case with dishwashers, but you can now change the front panels in some of the larger fridge-freezers as well.

◪ *High gloss luxury*

This luxurious option has a white lacquer finish with a smooth sheen. The elegant moulding on the panels gives the kitchen a smart image.

Wooden door fronts come painted, stained or varnished. Which you choose depends on just how vibrant and colourful a kitchen you'd like. There are other effects which work well on wood. Try them yourself or seek out a ready-finished unit. If you are buying ready-finished doors, make sure the whole lot is delivered at the same time, as colours may vary between batches.

Liming defines the graining on wood with a white wax. It works best on more open grained timbers such as pine and oak.

Staining plain wood adds colour and helps to even out the tone of overly knotty or deeply grained wood.

Stencilling patterns or designs on to plain or panelled doors instantly revamps worn kitchen units by adding extra colour.

Highlighting or **outlining** the shaping of panelled doors with stains or paint adds depth and colour to the doors.

Marbling, ragging and colour washing are all effective treatments for kitchen doors.

Once you add a layer of paint to a door or drawer front you run the risk of chipping, so seal the surface properly with lacquer or varnish. If the desired finish totally covers the door then consider choosing ones made of MDF instead of solid wood. They are cheaper and provide a better surface for the paint.

◩ *Stained oak*
The inky-blue stain on the surface of these door and drawer fronts brings out the natural grain of the oak and gives the kitchen an up-to-the-minute look.

◩ *Shaker style*
Painted wood is always a good option for a stylish kitchen. The teal blue painted units here do much to create the room's authentic Shaker look.

HANDLES

Once you've decided on the units, you can add the finishing touch with suitable door handles. Chrome, brass, steel, coloured, wood, plastic, and porcelain types are available. These come in various styles – knob, integrated or bar style. If possible try out your chosen door with a number of alternative handles at the showroom, before making your final choice. If there are none you like, ask the manufacturer to supply the doors without holes and add your own handles. You can then visit other manufacturers to see their ranges or even improvise with whatever original device catches your eye.

◪ *Hands on*
Handles come in all sorts of shapes and sizes. It's worth taking your time to find the type that complements your choice of units.

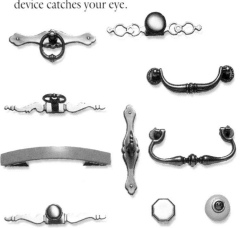

KITCHEN SINKS

The sink is an essential working part of the kitchen, so it makes sense to think carefully about the size, shape, colour and material you want before you buy.

The sink plays an important part in the overall efficiency of the kitchen, linking food preparation, food storage and cooking. It is used for all sorts of everyday tasks, ranging from preparation of fresh foods to hand washing clothes. Even if you have a dishwasher, a roomy, easy to clean sink is still essential, not just for food preparation but also for washing delicate items such as crystal or large items such as roasting tins.

To choose a new sink from the wide range of styles and materials available you need to know which type suits your particular needs.

These days, many sinks are designed as work centres, complete with chopping boards, strainers, extra drainers and even waste disposal units. Alternatively, if you spend less time in the kitchen or have a separate utility room you may opt for a simple single bowl.

On the following pages you can read about the wide choice of sink materials on the market, from traditional fireclay to modern polycarbonates and composite materials. Taps also need careful thought, whether you go for ones in a metal finish or in the same colour as the sink.

This stainless steel one and a half bowl sink is built into the worktop infront of the window. A plastic strainer unit in the half bowl collects any debris making light work of cleaning up after food preparation.

MATERIALS

Several different materials are used for making kitchen sinks. Choice depends on whether or not you want a coloured sink, what you want to use it for and the amount you want to pay.

STAINLESS STEEL

Stainless steel is hard wearing, easy to clean and preferred by professional cooks. Sinks come in either a matt, shiny or textured finish and are usually sold with accessories, including chopping boards and baskets. Stainless steel sinks are made in all shapes and sizes, including double, one and a half and single bowls and corner models. It is possible to buy a complete professional stainless steel worktop system with inset sinks. Steel is heat and impact resistant, but can be scratched.

ENAMEL

If you want a coloured sink to match your kitchen decor, enamel is the perfect choice. Enamel used to be the main material for sink manufacture, but because it chipped easily it was gradually replaced by harder wearing stainless steel. If you want enamel, look for a brand which has a surface that is hard wearing and chip resistant.

CAST IRON

Cast iron sinks are popular in the USA, but have only just become available in the UK in a limited choice of colours. They are very hardwearing and have an attractive traditional look.

CERAMIC AND FIRECLAY

Ceramic and fireclay sinks are available in both traditional and modern designs. The old-fashioned deep butler or Belfast sink is the most popular, as it works well in a traditional kitchen. Modern style ceramic sinks are available in a choice of colours including cream, ivory, mocha, beige, grey, graphite and black.

ARTIFICIAL STONE

Artificial stone – of which Corian is the best known – is a mix of minerals and polymers. The sinks can be welded seamlessly into lengths of worktop, giving smooth, unbroken lines. It comes in a choice of plain colours or stone effects and is heat, scratch and impact resistant.

COMPOSITE MATERIALS

Composites are basically a blend of quartz silica and acrylic resins. Those with 'granit' in the name include rock chips in the mix. The material is incredibly hardwearing and is both heat and impact resistant.

Some materials can be very difficult to keep clean. The worst offenders are those with a slightly textured surface which provides a trap for limescale. This in turn provides a surface for liquids such as red wine, tea and coffee to cling to. Look for a really smooth surface to avoid this problem.

POLYCARBONATE

Polycarbonate is the cheapest of all coloured sink materials. It is a type of plastic and although it is chip and scratch resistant, it can be damaged by heat, so avoid putting very hot pans on the draining board. The colours normally available are white, cream, mocha, cappuccino and beige.

▲ The traditional option
This Belfast ceramic sink suits a country style setting and looks good surrounded by rustic striped pine units and work surfaces. An antique brass mixer tap completes the look.

▼ Custom made Corian
This Corian double bowl sink comes complete with a drainage area, but is separate from the rest of the worktop, so you can have a Corian sink in conjunction with, say, laminate or granite surfaces in the rest of the

WASTE DISPOSERS

A waste disposer grinds food waste (including bones) into small particles which are then flushed into the drains. Bear in mind that you can't use a waste disposer if you have a septic tank or cesspit, as the protein in the waste upsets the delicate biological balance in the tank.

If you want a waste disposer, make sure the sink can be cut to house it. This isn't possible on some ceramic and fireclay sinks.

▲ Single bowl simplicity
The single bowl sink and drainer here, in a silica-based composite material, comes with a coordinating large bowl basket and gold mixer taps.

◀ Two is company
Two round stainless steel single bowl sinks set into an extra wide laminate worktop do the job of a modern work centre sink. A rack suspended over the sinks takes the place of a more conventional drainer.

SHAPE AND SIZE

The shape and size of sink you choose naturally depends on the space you have available. Bowl depth varies too, so make sure you end up with a sink that is too shallow for your washing up and food preparation needs. Most sinks are not deep enough to allow you to fit a bucket beneath the tap, or to wash large oven or baking trays – Belfast and butler sinks are the exception. If you have a utility room, it is worth buying a deep sink for this room in addition to a smaller sink in the kitchen.

For the sake of your back, make sure the sink is positioned at the right height. You should be able to reach the bottom of the bowl without bending.

SINGLE BOWL AND DRAINER
Measuring 980 x 500mm (38 ½ x 19 ¾in), this sort of sink is suitable for installation in a 500mm (20in) base unit. You can position the drainer on either the right or left side of the sink and plumb a dishwasher or washing machine under the draining side.

ONE AND A HALF BOWL
This sort of sink has a large bowl separated from the drainer by a smaller, shallow half bowl and is suitable for installation in a 600mm (24in) base unit. Although most one and a half bowl sinks are the same length as single bowl, single drainer models, you can't fit a dishwasher or washing machine completely beneath the drainer because the smaller bowl is in the way. The smaller bowl is useful for defrosting frozen foods and for washing vegetables.

DOUBLE BOWL
Double bowl sinks are designed for installation in a 1000mm (40in) base unit. The sink can have two bowls with a small central shallow bowl in the middle, or two bowls with a drainer at one side.

BUILT-UNDER SINKS
Built-under sinks are single or double bowls designed to be inset into a stone, artificial stone or wooden worktop. The top at either side of the sink is grooved to make a drainer. Belfast and butler sinks are built under.

CORNER SINKS
This type of sink is shaped to fit diagonally across a corner and is a useful option where space is short. Corner sinks can have a large single bowl and a drainer or a one and a half bowl with a smaller drainer.

MULTI-BOX SINKS
Multi-box sinks are fitted with a lidded waste chute which connects to a bag or waste bin below the sink. Food leftovers and vegetable peelings can be scraped straight into the chute from the plate or chopping board, safely out of the reach of pets or children.

◢ *A dark and handsome kitchen A one and a half bowl sink in stainless steel with a coordinating mixer tap is the height of elegance when combined with a drainer and worktop in black to match the black ash kitchen units.*

KITCHEN TAPS

Kitchen sinks are designed for use with a centrally mounted mixer tap with a swivelling spout. Taps can be the same colour as the sink or in a metal finish. Antique finish mixers are available for use with a traditional style sink.

As your hands are inevitably wet or slippery at times, easy to use controls are important in the kitchen. You can turn quarter turn and single lever mixer taps on and off with fingertip pressure.

If you live in an area where drinking water has a poor flavour, think about fitting a water purifier underneath the sink. The purifier removes nitrates, chlorine, minerals and unpleasant tastes and smells from drinking water. It can be connected to an extra small tap mounted on the sink, or to a special three way mixer which dispenses hot, cold and drinking water through separate outlets.

A tap fitted with a flexible hose which can be stretched to fill a bucket or used to rinse the sink bowl thoroughly is well worth thinking about. (In the UK, make sure you choose one which is suitable for use with UK unbalanced water pressure. Some imported flexi-taps can only be used in systems where hot and cold water are at the same balanced pressure.)

◀ *Coping with corners*
This stainless steel one and a half bowl sink is specially designed to make full use of a kitchen corner. It comes with all mod cons – a stainless steel drainer rack that fits over the large bowl; a colander for the half bowl and a flexible hose attachment for the tap that makes light of washing up and food preparation.

◢ *High gloss enamel*
Made from cast iron with an enamelled finish, this two and a half bowl sink is an attractive high gloss addition to the kitchen.

◀ *Underbuilt for elegance*
This stainless steel round bowl sink is underbuilt into a wooden work surface for understated glamour.

35

ACCESSORIES

All modern sinks come with accessories which may be sold separately or as a complete package with the sink and taps. Package deals are normally better value for money than buying the items separately.

Basket set One or two plastic or metal baskets which sit either inside the bowl or on the drainer, these are useful for draining plates and for washing vegetables.

Central strainer basket This is a plastic or steel basket with a perforated base which sits inside the central bowl. Useful for defrosting foods, as melted ice goes straight down the drain.

Chopping board Either hardwood or a dense plastic, the chopping board is designed to fit over the bowl, turning the sink into a useful extra worktop area.

Drainer tray This perforated plastic tray is designed to sit on the drainer of a stainless steel sink to prevent items resting directly on the steel surface. It adds colour but is not worth paying extra for.

Pop-up waste Replacing the traditional plug and chain, the pop-up waste opens or closes by twisting a knob on the front of the sink.

Soap dispenser Liquid soap is held in a reservoir under the sink and dispensed straight into the bowl at the touch of a button. You can use it for washing up liquid.

Strainer waste This catches food waste so it doesn't get into the waste pipe. A strainer waste is standard on most sinks.

◤ A workcentre sink

This stainless steel one and a half bowl corner sink is ideal for food preparation. You can clean vegetables in the large bowl, for example, then keep them submerged in water in the half bowl. The sink even includes a rubbish chute and under-sink waste bin.

◀ Coordinating extras

If your sink doesn't come with accessories, you can buy them separately to coordinate with your kitchen decor. This pine plate drainer is ideal for a country style kitchen.

◥ Sink accessories

This stainless steel sink comes complete with a wire basket, chopping board and strainer bowl.

EATING IN THE KITCHEN

The kitchen is more than just a place to prepare and cook food. Even if you have a separate dining room, the convenience of everyday eating in the kitchen is hard to resist.

I n many households today, families sit down together around the dining room table only once or twice a week. As lifestyles become more relaxed, the trend is towards light meals, snacks and family suppers in the kitchen.

People who think of entertaining as a chance to relax with friends and family often prefer the more casual setting of the kitchen. Dishes can be served straight to the table without the need for trays and trolleys. And, instead of labouring over the preparation and cooking away from your guests, you can enjoy their company while you work.

There are many advantages to light meals for the family in the kitchen. Breakfasts can be served and cleared away speedily. Young children can be fed and supervised in an area that is easily cleaned. Teenagers who like to grab their food and run and families where everyone seems to come in hungry at a different time of day can be catered for with the minimum of fuss. Busy working couples can relax over a simple supper and older people can cut down on unnecessary journeys between kitchen and dining room.

Not every kitchen is large enough to accommodate a farmhouse table and enough chairs for the family, but there are simple ways to economize on space that allow a more than adequate eating area without skimping on comfort.

Eating in the kitchen needn't be a rushed affair. If there's room for a separate table and chairs, an attractively presented breakfast table encourages the family to sit down together at the start of a busy day.

KITCHEN OPTIONS

There are three basic options for an eating area in the kitchen: a built-in countertop dining surface when space is at a premium; fixed banquette seating with a free-standing table in an alcove or corner; or, space permitting, a separate table and chairs in their own area.

COUNTERTOPS

Modern kitchen designs offer plenty of scope for creativity when it comes to eating arrangements and are the best solution to creating space for eating in a very small kitchen. As well as the traditional, straight breakfast bar with a couple of stools tucked underneath, manufacturers of fitted kitchens produce a range of countertops designed specifically for informal dining. Rounded or angular, they can be positioned at the end of peninsular storage units or free-standing island work spaces, or they can project into the room at right angles to a run of units along the walls. An island unit or a counter with a width of at least 46cm (18in) and a depth of 36cm (14in) is sufficient for casual meals and snacks for one person. Other points to bear in mind include:

❖ The standard kitchen unit work surface is higher than the normal dining table. Bar stools or other high-level seats are fine for adults, but choose stools with arms and high footrest bars for young children.

❖ The number of people who can fit around the dining area together varies according to size and design, but it makes for a feeling of companionship if two people can sit at right angles.

❖ It is much more pleasant to eat at a counter that faces into a room or looks out of a window than to eat at one that faces a blank wall. If necessary, liven up the wall with a poster or prints.

❖ Open shelves above a counter used for eating are friendlier than closed cupboards.

❖ A plant or a vase of flowers on the counter provides an instant centrepiece.

▼ *An island unit is ideal for light meals if the room is big enough for people to move around without disturbing anyone seated. In this handsome scheme, white tiling defines the eating area.*

▲ *This breakfast bar at one end of a peninsular unit neatly separates the preparation and eating areas. An under-counter recess allows a comfortable amount of leg room and space to store the stools out of the way when they are not needed.*

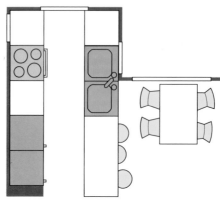

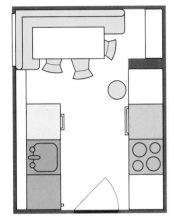

▶ *If there's a spare alcove or corner of a room, banquette seating makes the most of limited space. Here, attractive cushions on the seats and chairs, a matching rug, prints on the walls and special lighting all help set a relaxed dining mood.*

BANQUETTE SEATING

Built-in, upholstered bench seating is used in restaurants for a very good reason – more people can squeeze in than at separate tables and chairs.

The arrangement works in a similar way in the home, making good use of space, especially in an alcove, corner or recess. Storage can be incorporated under flip-up seating to make the most of small rooms.

The sense of enclosure that banquette seating gives is pleasingly cosy and has the added bonus of keeping energetic children in place. Seating can be L-shaped, on two facing sides, or U-shaped, with perhaps an extra chair pushed up to the end of the table when needed. Choose banquette tables with a single central support or the kind of cross-over legs that do not make getting in and out difficult.

Although purpose-built banquette seating is expensive, many cheaper alternatives are possible. You can improvise with garden seats, settles or even old church pews, softened with cushions on the seats and for back rests. Remember when you are measuring up for the seat cushions to leave enough space between the seat and the underside of the table for a generous amount of leg room. Choose a practical fabric and filling that is easily washable.

Separate Tables

A small table is often the simplest and most versatile way to create an eating space in the kitchen, provided that there is enough room. Even the smallest table provides somewhere to sit, turning a kitchen into more than an area to prepare food. If you haven't enough worktop space, choose a small table that can double as a food preparation area, where you can sit and work.

Make sure you leave enough room to walk past the table, especially if there's a route through to another room or the garden. It's also important to be able to reach the sink, the oven and the fridge without making anyone move.

A circular table can accommodate extra seats more easily than a rectangular one but when not in use it takes up more room, as it cannot be pushed up against a wall or into a corner. Pick one with fold down wings if space is tight. Choosing a fold down table and fold up chairs allows the furniture to be stacked out of the way when not in use, freeing the space for other purposes.

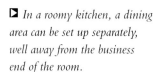

▲ With its cut-away tabletop, this custom-made generous-sized table does not interrupt the flow of work in the kitchen.

▶ In a roomy kitchen, a dining area can be set up separately, well away from the business end of the room.

◀ An ingenious design of triangular seats and table, and a couple of extra chairs, can be fitted into the smallest of spaces – this arrangement seats four but takes up next to no space when not in use.

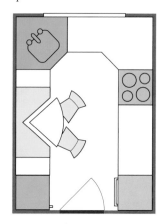

BOUNDARIES

Use different flooring in the two areas. A non-slip rug or carpet will dress up the eating area so that it seems more like a dining room. Make use of plants and flowers to give a relaxed atmosphere and distract attention from the work area.

❖ Lighting is an instant way to switch the emphasis when the meal is ready. Dimmed lights over the work area with a pendant light or downlighter over the eating area, or a table lamp on the work surface, can change the mood instantly.

❖ Aim to create a space that is not blasted by heat from the cooker or suffused by cooking smells. A fan in the cooker hood helps to draw steam and odours away, either by filtering or extracting the air.

❖ Try to create a division between the cooking and eating areas so that you are not confronted by a sink full of dirty pans when you sit down to eat.

❖ A peninsular or island unit works well as a room divider and can serve as a sideboard. Open ladder-type shelves or blinds can be used as effective screens.

◨ *A separate table and chairs work particularly well in a traditional style of kitchen. The marble top on this café-style table makes a useful extra work surface.*

41

SPACE SAVERS

It helps if there is plenty of space for a table in the kitchen, but there are many ways to create a small eating area. The most versatile designs use one surface to double as a work surface and eating area, but other tables ingeniously pull down or out or slide round to provide an instant but temporary eating corner.

❖ **Gateleg or other folding table** A versatile traditional standby, a gateleg table has one or two leaves that fold down flat when not in use.

❖ **Flap table** Ideal for a quick breakfast or simple supper for one or two people, a small, semicircular table fixed to the wall hinges down to extend no further than a narrow shelf when not in use.

❖ **Pull-out table** Designed by fitted kitchen manufacturers, these tables can be pulled out from under a counter or from a cupboard. When pushed back, the edge of the table is indistinguishable from a drawer front. When open, it provides a surface large enough for a two- or occasionally four-place setting.

❖ **Fold-ups and hang-ups** Chairs and stools that fold up and can be stacked neatly out of the way, or even hung on the wall or behind a door are the ultimate space savers.

❖ **Bar stools** Stools or seats with very low backs can be pushed right under the countertop at the end of a meal.

❖ **Stow-away units** There are some ingenious tables with fold-down leaves that incorporate a built-in storage facility for a set of matching folding chairs.

◩ *Though sociable, a round table is not the most space saving of shapes – this semicircular banquette makes the most of the bay while accommodating the table.*

◩ *A simple white countertop flap, made inviting with a jug of flowers, is perfectly in keeping with a stylish modern kitchen.*

▶ *When space is tight the cook can still enjoy a midday break seated at this space-saving drawer-fronted table flap.*

ROOM TO DINE

A separate dining room may not always be possible or desirable – so how do you set about finding space for family and friends to meet and dine together in comfort?

In today's smaller homes and with the busy lifestyle of most families, it is tempting to make do with a table in the kitchen or living room. But even if the whole family eats together only occasionally and you entertain rarely, your dining area needs to be practical and comfortable.

Eating should be an enjoyable experience, a time for families to sit down together, if possible at least once a day. Balancing a tray on your lap in front of the television, or making do with a breakfast bar for anything but the lightest of snacks, is no way to enjoy food on a regular basis – it also destroys the social aspect of family meals.

Like the old parlour, the formal dining room has declined in recent decades, victim not only of more informal social habits but also of the growing need for a limited number of rooms to serve several purposes. And unless it is conveniently situated and frequently used, a formal dining room can be a cold, depressing place, dominated by an imposingly large table surrounded by uncomfortable chairs.

What are the alternatives? Unless your lifestyle includes regular entertaining, most family dining rooms can double for other uses, such as a home office/study. Alternatively, you can establish a dining area in the kitchen or at one end of the living room. The most flexible plan of all is to eat different meals in different areas, depending on your family's needs.

Though the room may be small, dining space in the kitchen can still be attractive and comfortable, particularly for light meals.

43

DINING CHOICE

A separate dining room allows you to escape entirely from everything and relax over a meal. For maximum convenience, the room should be close to the kitchen. If your existing dining room is under used, consider flexible alternatives – could the space do double duty, perhaps as a study? If the room is downright inconvenient, use it for something else and eat elsewhere – in a kitchen/diner or living room/diner, for example.

A kitchen/diner has a relaxed informal atmosphere, with immediate access to cooking areas, food, cutlery and china – though not all cooks like to dine in the workplace. A fairly large room is essential. To accommodate a good-sized wooden table in a family kitchen you will need at least 4 x 5m (13 x 16ft) of floor space. Depending on the layout, you may be able to partition off the dining area, perhaps with a countertopped unit that doubles as a breakfast bar. Lighting should be comfortable to the eye, with any glare shielded.

A living room/diner works well in a through room where a central dividing wall has been removed. If possible have the dining area at the end nearest to the kitchen. You may be able to make a hatchway through for easier serving and clearing.

A dual purpose room is worth considering if you don't want to set aside a separate room and the more usual options aren't possible. Think about a study/diner, where the table doubles as a desk, or have a folding table and a sofa bed in a dining/guest room. Include plenty of storage so the room can change roles easily.

A conservatory makes a wonderful dining area on a warm evening, but it can become too hot in summer and too cold in winter. Restrict dining there to the warmer months and fit blinds if the area is too hot.

An upstairs room with a view, or one that's light and sunny, has beautiful windows or simply appeals to you in some way, is a real treat if one of your main pleasures is to linger over a meal. The sense of well being will far outweigh the possible inconvenience of a dining area at some remove from the kitchen.

Movable feasts, with different meals taken in different situations, are a flexible possibility. For breakfast, it's pleasant to have a folding table in the corner of a room that catches the morning sun; use the designated dining room or dining area – which can also be used for other purposes – for weekend lunch, evening meals and dinner parties; a pull-out table or countertop in the kitchen often works well for light meals; tea, traditionally taken in the sitting room, can be served in a garden room, conservatory or on the patio in the summer.

◪ *A combined living/dining room often works best if the different roles occupy separate areas. One of the simplest ways of dividing the space is to use a double-sided freestanding shelf unit, on which can be stored the accessories most appropriate to each of the two facing areas.*

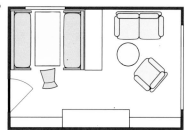

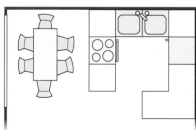

◀ *A dining area that can be dressed up for special occasions, yet still serves the everyday needs of the family, is a flexible scheme that works well for most households.*

▲ *In this stylish scheme a peninsular arm divides the space, while colour coordinated soft furnishings and pictures establish a separate identity for dining.*

▲ *A room that leads off the kitchen makes good practical sense for a dining area. Access should be convenient – a serving hatch is worth considering if you haven't a through-way like the one here.*

DRAW UP A PLAN

If you are moving into a new house or flat, or have decided for family reasons to re-assess living arrangements, it's a good idea to draw up a plan – preferably to a simple scale – and play around with alternatives. This is what architects and designers start off with, and it's surprising how seeing your house laid out on paper can prompt alterations which you would never have thought of before. By removing a wall, or part of a wall, you might be able to bring another area into the kitchen. Or you could find that the kitchen itself can be planned more efficiently, to provide an extra area for family eating in space previously taken up by fixtures and fittings. If you decide on any structural alterations, check with an expert whether the work is structurally feasible and get several estimates to assess the cost.

ROOM FOR COMFORT

A homemaker can learn a lot from restaurants. Nothing is more disturbing to eating comfort than being in a passage route, whether at home or out. Caterers find that in fairly large restaurants the side tables are taken first, the least popular being island tables near the entrance or the swing doors into the kitchen.

The same principle applies at home: you don't want to have to pull in your chair to let your neighbour past to make coffee. An adjacent wall is nice to lean on, too, and gives a feeling of security – diners in restaurant booths don't take the outside seats first.

◄ *A well planned modern home has a separate dining area with direct access to the kitchen, which is ideal for family meals and more formal entertaining.*

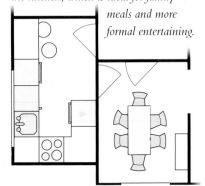

▲ *Create a pleasant place to linger over a meal by making the most of an existing asset, such as a handsome window, a fine view or a sunny corner. A few potted pelargoniums by this window gives the area a conservatory feel.*

PLANNING A SMALL KITCHEN

*A well planned layout that allows adequate space for units,
other storage and appliances helps to make the best use of the limited
area available in a small kitchen.*

A t no time is careful planning in the home more critical than when designing or refurbishing a very small kitchen. Squeezing in enough working and storage space is a real test of ingenuity, so throughout the planning stage look through as many kitchen and appliance brochures as possible for ideas.

Before you actually start work, take some time to think about how you use your kitchen. You definitely need preparation, cooking, serving and dishwashing areas, but if you live in a small flat you may want to fit in a small eating space as well.

Consider the appliances and utensils you need to make room for and how best to include them, while leaving the maximum amount of work space free.

Combined ovens and microwaves save on space and there are many slimline dishwashers or washing machines that you can squeeze into tight corners.

Fitting enough kitchen units into a small kitchen is a problem. You can opt for custom-made units to make the most of the space available, but this tends to be expensive. An alternative is to use standard base and wall units and incorporate corner units with pull-out carousels for extra storage.

Worktop space in a small kitchen is necessarily limited, so make the most of what you have. Add extra shelving and storage where possible to store items such as toasters, storage jars and food processors that would otherwise clutter up work surfaces.

Small-scale appliances make the most of the space in this tiny kitchen, while the glass-fronted wall units keep crockery and glassware on view and help to create a sense of spaciousness.

A TIGHT FIT

There are many ways to create extra storage space in a confined kitchen. You can fit mid-way shelving systems in the unused space between the wall units and the worktop. These shelves relieve the work surface of items like storage jars, herbs and spices and small appliances. Hanging racks or hooks fitted at mid level can help to store essential kitchen utensils.

Kitchen units now come with storage facilities such as pull-out baskets or carousel units in corner cupboards to use all available space. You can fit small waste bins on sliding or pull-out rails under sink units. Alternatively, you can cut a piece out of your worktop, replace it with a flat hinged lid and place the bin underneath.

You can also include ingenious, foldaway ironing boards into drawer units and store appliances such as food processors on pull-out hinged shelves.

To use every last bit of space, you can put a storage unit in the often forgotten plinth area below the base units and use it to store large pans and trays or even a step ladder that allows you to reach high-up shelves. Alternatively, slot a floor heater into this space to keep the kitchen warm.

Hinged doors take up space when open, so dispense with them altogether or replace them with either sliding or bi-fold doors. You could even remove part of the wall around the door to create a wider opening into a dining room.

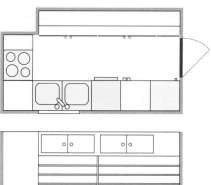

STYLISH FINISH

Once you've decided on the basic plan for your kitchen, you need to think about what style you want to create. A modern, streamlined kitchen with washable laminate units is particularly suited to a small space, but you can create an equally effective traditional look with oak or maple wood units.

The natural inclination with a small kitchen is to use pale, neutral colours to reflect light and give the impression of more space. Also, if you decorate the walls to blend rather than contrast with worktops and units the room appears larger than it actually is. To prevent blandness

creeping in, highlight details like handles and trims and add colourful accessories.

A fully tiled kitchen is easy to keep clean – an important consideration, as walls tend to get dirtier in a confined space. Avoid tiles with strong patterns and choose subtle striped effects or gently mottled designs instead. Rectangular tiles laid widthways across a narrow floor visually enlarge the floor space.

Integrating all machines in the kitchen behind door fronts that match your kitchen units gives the room a sleeker, more streamlined appearance as well as reducing noise.

SPACE-SAVING FIXTURES

Fitting all the basic equipment into a tiny kitchen requires careful thought, but finding space for all today's time-saving gadgets as well as a well-stocked larder is a real challenge – but don't despair, it can be done.

A combined oven/microwave can look after all your cooking needs and save on space at the same time. Alternatively, choose compact gas or electric cooking rings to fit into the worktop, place a single oven underneath and hang a small microwave at mid-height underneath a wall cupboard. Fitting a hinged cover over the rings is a good way to increase worktop space.

Even in a tiny kitchen, you still need to store adequate amounts of food, so don't underestimate the size of fridge or freezer you need. If you go for a smaller option, there are combined under-counter fridge-freezers that fit into a 45cm (17¾in) space or matching fridge and freezer units that sit in a 90cm (35½in) space. If you want a much larger freezer you can always site it somewhere else in the home – under the stairs or in a hall cupboard, for instance.

Dishwashers, washing machines, dryers and combined washer/dryers are now available in slimline widths of around 45cm (17¾in) as well as the conventional 60cm (23½in). A dishwasher may seem a luxury, but is useful for loading away dirty crockery when space beside the sink is minimal.

A sink with a half-width drainer slots easily into a worktop. You can make the sink area work for you with removable extras such as chopping boards and loose drainers, which you place over the sink to give more room for preparation and washing up. Neat corner sinks make use of an awkward space.

◀ *Open shelves set against the end of the run of units provide accessible storage for everyday crockery, while the shelf across the top of the window gives space for less frequently used items. The tiles are both a practical and decorative choice.*

▼ *There's room for everything in this small kitchen – even a built-in breakfast table. The table is semi-circular so you don't need to worry about sharp corners.*

◀ *Completely clutter-free, this narrow galley kitchen appears much larger than it actually is. A wall of floor-to-ceiling storage on the right keeps everything out of sight.*

▼ *This is the perfect solution if you don't have room for a separate kitchen. Arranged against one wall of the living/dining room, this galley kitchen can be hidden away behind bi-fold doors when not in use.*

LIGHT EFFECTS

Lighting is especially important in a small kitchen. A well and warmly lit kitchen has a more welcoming feel to it and a greater sense of spaciousness – strong lighting stops dark corners crowding in on you. Beware of harsh shadows, though. Background lighting should create a bright, soft overall effect. Wall-mounted spotlights angled upwards or uplighters on the top of wall cupboards wash light on to the ceiling to create a gentle feel.

Additional task lighting in the form of striplights underneath shelves, wall cupboards and the cooker extract hood gives you a good level of light for cooking and food preparation. Lighting inside deep wall or base units makes keeping your kitchen cupboards organized a simpler task.

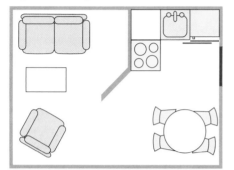

▲ *Tucked away in the alcove of an open-plan living room, this tiny kitchen combines practicality with streamlined good looks. The full-sized larder is hidden behind bold red doors – extra doors slide across to close off the end wall completely. A large wall mirror in the dining area gives the impression of more space.*

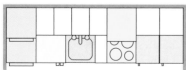

▲ *The run of units along this kitchen wall encompasses everything you need in a kitchen – and more – and manages to do it in a small area. Small-scale appliances are lined up beside cupboards, while shelves and drawers of various sizes use up any remaining room that would otherwise be lost.*

PLANNING A DIY KITCHEN

You can save a great deal of money by installing your new kitchen yourself, but be prepared for a lot of careful planning both before and during the work.

M ost kitchen unit suppliers sell rigid (pre-assembled) or flat-pack (self-assembly) units which you install yourself. It is sensible to have some professional help in planning the layout, but you can do a lot of the fitting yourself.

The main skill involved in installing a kitchen is woodworking – which is why many professional kitchen fitters were originally carpenters and joiners. But you may need to combine woodworking with decorating skills, at least some degree of electrical skill and, perhaps, plumbing skills too. If this is too daunting a prospect for you, bear in mind that you don't have to do everything yourself. You can always employ tradesmen to do those tasks you don't feel confident enough to do.

The finished kitchen depends not only on the time and care you take in planning the work but in how thorough you are in carrying it out. In particular, this means making sure that you fit all units with their sides vertical – not always easy on an uneven floor – and that worktops are truly horizontal, which is essential to make sure that a sink drains efficiently, for example.

Much of the detailed, fiddly work – and some of your mistakes – can be hidden away. Do, however, take special care when finishing off tasks: for example, tiling, sealing behind sinks and worktops, fitting end panels, laying floorcovering, and installing lighting under cupboards.

If you take all the points in this feature into consideration, you should be looking at an economical and a satisfying piece of work that lasts every bit as long and looks just as good as a kitchen installed by a full-time professional.

The vertical spacing of the units in this elegant kitchen is fixed by the oven housing and tall larder unit on the left. The cupboards above the peninsular unit are held up by a wall support pack.

TAKING MEASURE

It's best to think of a new kitchen in metric units. The dimensions of all new kitchen units are described in millimetres and you do not want to spend hours converting them all.

Kitchen wall and base units come in standard widths: 300, 400, 500, 600, 800 and 1000mm from side to side. Base units are usually 575mm deep (front to back) and 880mm high; wall units are about 320mm deep and either 600mm or 720mm high. Worktops come in 3m lengths – any run longer than 3m means you need a join. You have to join worktops where they meet at a corner in any case.

The standard worktop height is 900mm, which suits most people, with a gap of about 500mm between the top of the worktop and the underside of the wall cupboards. Some manufacturers make spice racks or mid-range units to fit in this gap, but in most kitchens it is tiled, so it helps if the gap is the height of an exact number of tiles – say, three 150mm tiles or four 108mm tiles. If you have tall units – built-in oven housings, for example – the gap is a fixed measurement.

Because of the fixed sizes of units, you are usually left with some odd gaps to fill between base units. There may be space to fit a 150mm wide wine rack, but the normal solution is to create a tray space with an infill unit, cut down to the size of the gap, with a towel rail attached to the underside of the worktop above. You don't usually have these sorts of problems with wall units as walls are usually broken up by windows. If there is a gap, however, you can fill it with a matching filler panel.

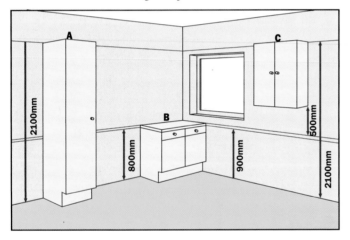

◣ *Some of the most useful pieces for your kitchen include a tall unit for brushes, mops and household cleaners, (**A**) a unit with drawers for crockery and kitchen utensils (**B**) and a high wall cupboard for groceries (**C**).*

▷ *Glass-fronted cupboards are no more complicated to assemble than their plainer counterparts and offer many decorative possibilities.*

FITTING OPTIONS

With the advances in kitchen unit design, few people would even consider building their own kitchen units from scratch. Although the materials are fairly cheap and readily available, you cannot cut them as accurately or as cleanly as kitchen unit manufacturers can on a machine. Homemade units are also much more difficult to join together than ready-made units.

The advantages of using pre-assembled rigid units are obvious: there's no need to worry about assembly and the units are often more robust than flat-pack units. There are two main disadvantages however. Rigid units are generally more expensive than flat packs, and they are more awkward to store before you fit them.

Most people opt for flat-pack units, which you assemble as you install them – all the screws and fittings are provided, and all the holes for screws and hinges are pre-drilled.

Flat-pack and rigid units vary in quality, depending largely on cost. It aids installation if adjustable legs are supplied with the units. These make the job easier if the floor is uneven, and they also protect the units from water damage. Adjustable brackets are available for wall units so that you can line up all the units once they are fitted.

◁ *There is no reason why a sink should be put under a window. In this clean, refined and modern kitchen, it works perfectly well in the centre of the 'U' shape.*

◁ *A detailed plan shows many of the unit style options available and how to organize the arrangement of units and appliances in a generously proportioned fitted kitchen.*

KEY TO KITCHEN LAYOUT

A Base unit	**F** Floor end panels	**L** Wall end shelf units
B Adjustable feet	**G** Floor end shelf unit	**M** Cornice
C Under worktop oven unit	**H** Towel rails	**N** Pelmets
D Tall appliance housing unit	**I** Wall units	**O** Plinths
E Infill unit	**J** Extractor hood	**P** Internal accessories
	K Slim wall unit	**Q** Worktop

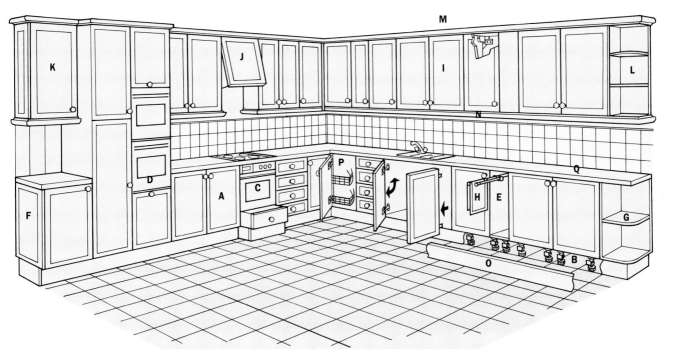

PLANNING POINTS

Your supplier can help you with planning your kitchen, but there are several points to bear in mind:

❖ Do allow worktop space either side of the sink and cooker
❖ Do position tall units at the end of a run
❖ Do fit plenty of electric sockets (but not over or too close to a cooker or sink)
❖ Don't position the cooking rings by a window, next to a door, in a corner or under a full-height wall unit
❖ Don't put a free-standing fridge and cooker side by side
❖ Don't position oven doors so that they open out on to room doors
❖ Don't fit a sink or inset cooking rings over a worktop join.

◨ *An 'L'-shaped arrangement of kitchen units has a tall unit at the end of the working area and a sink under a window, this makes the most efficient use of the space available.*

◨ *Fitting narrow units beside the oven ensures that all available space is used efficiently. Open wall end shelf units solve the problem of filling the space beside a window.*

◄ Well thought-out details – bottle shelves, spice drawers, fretwork cornice and extractor hood – combine style with practicality.

◄ Conflicts between unit doors and drawers at corners are hard to avoid. The last unit before the corner should be fitted with a carousel for optimum efficiency.

THE PLAN OF CAMPAIGN

If you are installing your own kitchen, make sure you have a clear plan of action – particularly if you need to continue cooking and washing up as normal while the work is in progress.

1. Before ripping out the old kitchen, install any new lighting and clean and repaint the ceiling.

2. Remove the old kitchen units – work in sections if you have to continue using the kitchen. If you need to level the floor, however, everything has to come out at once.

3. Install electrical wiring for any new socket outlets – with a solid-floor kitchen, the wires have to come down the wall – and alter the plumbing for sinks, washing machine and dishwasher. Install a vent for a tumble dryer at this stage if necessary.

4. Make walls sound. If they are in very bad condition, replaster them.

5. Level the floor with self-levelling floor compound, unless the floor is already exactly level. This makes unit and appliance fitting easier later on.

6. Cover the walls in your chosen paint or wallcovering, paying special attention to the areas that will show when the units are installed.

7. Draw out the worktop height and the positions of all of the wall units to make a final check on your plan.

8. Fit base units, making sure that they are exactly level – adjust the feet or use packing pieces where necessary. Next, secure them firmly to the wall. Put the main appliances, such as the oven and washing machine, in place at the same time.

9. Cut and fit the worktops, making any necessary cutouts for sinks and cooking rings. Call in a gas fitter to connect gas cooking rings and any other gas appliances. Seal all around the worktops with bathroom sealant.

10. Fit the wall cupboards, ensuring they are all at equal height above the worktop.

11. Do all the tiling.

12. Fit your chosen floor covering, taking it under the units, before fitting plinth boards.

There are two ways of neatening or finishing the end of an open run of units. One is to fit a decorative panel to match the doors of the units. The other, if there is room, is to fit a 300mm (12in) wide display unit with shelves. Both look better than a plain white end.

Along the tops of wall cupboards, you can fit wooden cornices. These come in lengths of three metres (10 feet) and provide a decorative finish which is more attractive than the plain white corner. Screw the cornice to the tops of the units, making sure you mitre the corners first.

Fit matching pelmets (decorative strips) along the bottom of the wall units in the same way, but this time secure them

with brackets. Fit under-cupboard strip lighting behind them to illuminate worktops.

Maximize storage space by fitting extra shelves, carousels in corner units, sliding wire baskets, door-mounted storage baskets, waste bins, spice racks, mid-range units, midway shelves, cutlery trays and so on. You can get all of these and other accessories by mail order if your kitchen supplier does not have them.

Finish by fitting plinth boards underneath the base units. With floor units, nail the boards to the unit with panel pins. If the units have adjustable feet, clip the plinths on – it makes them easier to remove. With some types of floor cover-

▲ *Pull-out towel rails that slot neatly into an infill unit mean you can tuck towels and drying cloths away out of sight under the worktop.*

▼ *An ordinary drawer front pulls out to reveal a table top that proves extremely useful as a space-saving breakfast bar or an extra work surface.*

▲ *Attractive and useful, an infill unit can comprise of storage for a few bottles of wine and a series of small drawers.*

▼ *Kitchen units fitted with adjustable legs are a good idea for uneven floors – or use a floor-levelling compound.*

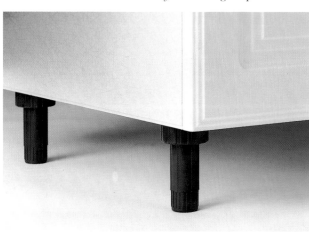

THE UNFITTED KITCHEN

The kitchen doesn't have to be a purely utilitarian space, dedicated solely to the preparation of food. An unfitted kitchen has a friendly feel that is just right for combining cooking, dining and living.

The unfitted or farmhouse kitchen is a look back to the past when the kitchen really was the heart of the home, with room to sit and relax as well as space for cooking. Today, more relaxed attitudes to eating and entertaining mean that many families prefer a multi-purpose space to a separate kitchen, dining and living room.

Family members often eat at different times, sometimes snacking, taking a meal while watching television or even studying, making a formal, separate dining room a little-used luxury. Choosing an unfitted kitchen complete with comfortable seating and work space creates a warm, welcoming centre for family life where cooking, eating, entertaining and activities such as hobbies or homework are all carried out.

Unlike a fully fitted kitchen, where the furniture and appliances need to be installed at the same time, an unfitted kitchen can evolve over the years. You can add unfitted elements gradually around a central core made up of the sink and cooker. Pieces can be old or new, but the style is essentially traditional.

In this unfitted kitchen the emphasis is centred on the dining area, with a huge table partially stained olive-green to coordinate with the dresser, wall-hung cabinet and kitchen units.

ESSENTIAL ELEMENTS

Although the unfitted kitchen is less formal in style than a fully fitted one, the basics of planning remain the same. You need to make sure that the cooking area, sink, working area and food storage area form a central work zone, so you can move quickly and easily from one to another.

An unfitted kitchen still has a core of fixed, essential items. These include the sink, dishwasher and washing machine which must be permanently connected to the water supply, the cooker, fridge and/or freezer. It is sensible to keep these working parts of the kitchen in one area, freeing the rest of the room for seating, storage and decorative furniture.

The sink is the centre of the working area. A deep Belfast sink built into a wooden, tiled or stone worktop is the traditional choice for an unfitted kitchen, but there's no reason why you shouldn't use stainless steel or a composite material built into a rustic-style 1m (39½in) base unit. You can even build a sink into an old pine sideboard or chest. A complete stainless steel worktop with an inset sink is another alternative for you to consider.

Tuck the dishwasher and washing machine away beneath the worktop, as close to the sink as possible to minimize pipe runs. You can hide the machines by fitting cupboard doors across the front or by running a curtain on a spring wire along the edge of the worktop.

You can choose either a fixed or a freestanding cooker for an unfitted kitchen. If your room has an old chimney breast or hearth, set the cooker or range into this alcove. You can give even built-in single ovens a traditional look by using two of them side by side with the cooking rings set into the work surface above. Fit cupboards or open shelves at either side of the ovens for pans and, if possible, conceal the extractor in the old chimney breast.

It is a good idea to draw a plan and jot down the relevant measurements – especially of awkward corners or alcoves. Keep it with you when you're out furniture hunting, so that if a dresser or cupboard catches your eye, you'll know at once if it fits the available space in your kitchen.

▽ *Open shelving and a dresser along one wall provide plenty of storage. Curtaining off more storage space and kitchen appliances beneath the L-shaped worktop gives the room an unsophisticated, country-fresh air.*

UNFITTED ADDITIONS

The real unfitted kitchen atmosphere comes from the pieces of freestanding furniture you add to the fixed elements to create a room you can use for everything from hobbies and homework to entertaining.

A large table suits all sorts of purposes from food preparation and serving meals to study, hobbies and other family activities. Pine is a favourite choice. Beware of very soft Croatian pine – it looks attractive and is reasonably priced but dents easily.

A couple of comfortable armchairs or a small sofa make a softer alternative to dining chairs when you want to relax rather than sit at the table. If there isn't enough space, think about building a window seat. Where there isn't room for extra seating, padded benches instead of dining chairs are a good idea. Alternatively, position the table in a corner and build a padded bench with storage space underneath along two of the walls.

Every kitchen needs storage space for food and utensils. A dresser is the favourite choice for a traditional unfitted kitchen. Dressers can combine both closed and visible storage and come in a variety of sizes, ranging from small double versions 120-150cm (4-5ft) long to massive farmhouse models 210-240cm (7-8ft) long. Measure the space available before you buy and remember that there must be enough room in front of the dresser to open doors and drawers. For flexible storage, choose a model with drawers and cupboards as well as open shelves. Although the dresser is an unfitted piece of furniture, you must attach the top part to the wall using flat metal clips before loading the shelves, otherwise it may become top heavy.

An old stripped pine wardrobe fitted with internal shelves is a good place to store less decorative kitchen equipment, such as baking trays and pans and tinned and packeted food. A sideboard with deep cupboards and drawers is another alternative. If you have the space, you can even build a larder across a corner or in a deep alcove. Site it on a north wall if possible, and install ventilation. Fit granite or slate shelves to keep foods cool.

◀ *In spite of its modern appliances, this kitchen has an old-fashioned feel, with its small pine dresser, wall-fixed shelves and small cabinet.*

LIGHTING

The unfitted kitchen is a multi-purpose room, so it is important to install lighting which is suitable for a variety of tasks. You need clear illumination above working areas and softer light for dining and relaxing.

For flexibility consider having ceiling-mounted directional low-voltage halogen lighting, combined with wall lights in the sitting area and a rise and fall fitting above the dining table – all these could be controlled by dimmer switches for added versatility.

◀ *Arranged around a central island, this large kitchen has a welcoming unfitted feel, with the large stripped wood dresser fitting neatly into an alcove. In the dining area a generously big farmhouse table can accommodate all sorts of family activities, from meals to homework or hobbies.*

VISIBLE STORAGE

Visible, easily accessible storage is one of the hallmarks of the traditional unfitted kitchen.

Open shelves Shelves can be wall-mounted or installed below a length of worktop. Those near cooking and preparation areas are ideal for frequently used ingredients and utensils. You can double the usefulness of shelves by attaching cup hooks along the front edge. Use these for mugs, jugs, bunches of herbs, garlic or utensils.

Use wicker baskets on widely spaced under-worktop shelves to store vegetables. If you prefer to hide the contents of the shelves, the simplest method is to run a curtain on a spring wire across the front.

Hanging storage A ceiling-mounted circular or rectangular utensil rack is a practical and useful addition above the main preparation area. You can hang jugs, sieves, small pans, egg baskets, bunches of herbs and strings of onions and garlic from S-shaped hooks, ready for instant use. You can also add a wall-mounted grid or rail to hold smaller utensils and jars of herbs and spices.

▶ *The antique plate rack above the butler sink is a charming addition to this unfitted kitchen. The base of an old sewing machine topped with a marble slab becomes a useful extra work surface, which can be stored underneath the draining board when not in use.*

▼ *A custom-built dresser painted cream to match the walls provides a mixture of open and closed storage in this kitchen. With inset ceramic tiles along the top of the cupboard, the dresser also serves as a work surface. Specially designed for worktop use, the tiles are hardwearing and heat resistant.*

▼ *The modern equivalent of a traditional butcher's block, this mobile work station is the perfect accessory for an unfitted kitchen. Ideal for food preparation, it includes a robust chopping board, a knife rack, storage for food and containers and a towel rail.*

ASSESSING A FITTED KITCHEN

Whether you're starting from scratch or simply revamping, the basics of any well organized kitchen are worked out at the initial planning stage.

F itted kitchens come in many styles and finishes but, essentially, there are three ways of buying them. If you are competent at DIY and want to keep costs down, you can buy the units from a large DIY store and install them yourself. You can also buy from direct-sell companies that advertise in monthly or Sunday supplement magazines. A representative from the company visits your home with brochures and door samples, and then organizes planning and fitting. Alternatively, you can go to a kitchen specialist whose business is planning, selling and installing kitchens, and who takes care of every aspect from start to finish. Although DIY stores, direct-sell companies and kitchen specialists should all plan your kitchen free

of charge and provide you with drawn up plans, professional fitting generally costs extra.

Whichever option you choose, avoid costly and frustrating mistakes by working out all your needs beforehand. However, there's more to planning a kitchen than simply measuring up and transferring the results to squared paper. It is a detailed job which calls for electrical and plumbing expertise, familiarity with the types of appliances and furniture available, and a vital dash of design flair.

Regardless of whether you want to leave everything to the professionals or take on some of the work yourself, you'll have a head start if you arm yourself with a comprehensive list of your needs and preferences before you go shopping.

These traditional panelled kitchen units are rigid – that is, they're sold already assembled for you or the manufacturer to install. The island, with its practical wooden worktop, double sink and lowered counter for eating, increases the efficiency of this kitchen.

A WORKABLE SOLUTION

Before choosing a furniture style or finish, consider the following all important basics as the framework of your kitchen plan. Keep a pad handy to list your ideas.

❖ **Working surface**s Clear areas of working space are essential. You need put-down space beside the oven and cooking top for hot dishes, and a preparation area near the sink. If space is tight consider a sink with a chopping board which fits over the bowl. If you prepare a lot of fresh foods, an inset chopping board or butcher's block is a good idea, while a marble, granite or smooth slate block is perfect for making and rolling pastry.

❖ **Storage** Don't think of kitchen storage just in terms of cupboards. Today's modern kitchen units are fitted with a wide selection of pull-outs for storing food, drinks, pans and cleaning materials. Provided your kitchen planner has details of your storage needs they will be able to choose the appropriate units and fittings for you. So make a complete list, including the amount of space you think is necessary for foods, the size and

number of pans and crockery you want to store, and any items you would like to keep to hand.

Storage must be easily accessible. This is where conventional wall cupboards present a problem. Most women of average height find it impossible to reach the upper shelves of a wall unit. One way round this is to have a set of folding pull-out steps fitted into the plinth below base units. Another option is to choose units where you can use every shelf without stretching or climbing. High board units, which don't go much above shoulder height, are a recent development in kitchen design and can be integrated with conventional base units to make an interesting, practical layout.

❖ **Lighting** A single overhead light is rarely the best way to illuminate a kitchen as you're always working in your own shadow. Halogen lights incorporated into the base of wall units or shelves cast an illuminating glow over work surfaces. One or two well placed spotlights also make the room more comfortable to work in.

◀ One cost saving option is to fit the kitchen yourself. This kitchen, with leaded glass display units and solid American oak doors is sold as a flat pack. If DIY is not your strong point, the manufacturer offers an optional fitting service.

▼ The compact layout of this kitchen illustrates the obvious advantage of having a kitchen custom-made. In a very small space, this plan manages to include a serviceable breakfast bar, a fully integrated fridge and dishwasher and plenty of work surfaces. Narrow cupboards right up to the ceiling provide maximum storage.

◀ Most manufacturers make units in a wide range of sizes. Here, narrow units alongside wider ones provide well thought-out storage for the chief requirements. Open shelving means frequently used saucepans and china are readily to hand.

▼ Some manufacturers offer a wider choice of unit sizes than others. This kitchen illustrates a clever use of units of different heights. Low units bring the cooker top down to a comfortable working level, while a taller unit raises the wall oven to a convenient height. A narrow unit left of the low ones makes maximum use of space.

Some homes have an oven, separate rings, microwave, fridge, freezer, dishwasher, washing machine and tumble dryer, but few have space to keep all of these in the kitchen.

Decide which of these are essential for you to have in your kitchen as opposed to a utility room or a garage. Remember the washing machine and dishwasher have to be sited near plumbing and the tumble dryer may need venting through an outside wall.

The size of appliances is also a consideration. Although the idea of a double oven is tempting, it is an expensive and often under-used buy. Think instead about a good quality single oven that is large enough for most families, plus a combination microwave. Slimline versions of appliances which measure only 45cm (18in) wide are a space-saving option for small kitchens.

Appliances can be freestanding, built in below the worktop or, in the case of an oven, at eye level so that a microwave can be fitted above or below it – a sensible way to use otherwise wasted space. Fridges and freezers can be positioned side by side or stacked one on top of the other to save floor space.

For a streamlined, fitted look consider fully integrated appliances which are fitted with doors to match units. Although they offer the same features as freestanding or ordinary built-in models from the same range, the price is much higher because they have to be made so that the kitchen doors fit on to them.

▲ *For a streamlined look, appliances like dishwashers, refrigerators and washing machines can be fully integrated behind doors that match the rest of the kitchen.*

▲ *Tucked into a corner, a generous fridge/freezer merges into the kitchen layout because its doors are attached to coordinating wooden doors. A system of pull-out baskets makes full use of the remaining deep but narrow cupboards.*

▶ *Some manufacturers offer a less costly solution to fully integrated units in which the front of an appliance is fitted with a laminated panel that coordinates with other units in the kitchen.*

STORAGE IN A NEW KITCHEN

Organizing what items go in which type of units is a fundamental part of a well-planned kitchen. Take time to consider your own individual storage needs, so that your new kitchen is an efficient place to work.

B uying a new kitchen gives you the ideal opportunity to choose storage units that are tailor-made to your needs. The kitchen is a storehouse for an enormous number of items, ranging from fresh foods to cleaning materials. Before you start planning your kitchen layout, work out what you have to store and where you want to keep everything.

You can bear your specific needs in mind as you choose your kitchen units from a wide range of modern wall units, drawer units, cupboards and midway or open shelving. There are also many special inserts that you can add to the basic units to expand their storage capacity. Then, when you organize the kitchen layout

systematically, you end up with a kitchen that is easy to keep tidy and efficient to work in.

Well-planned storage can save time and energy too. When you plan your storage arrangements round the cooking/preparation area so that frequently used utensils and foods are just a few steps away, you can reduce much of the effort required to cook and clean in the average kitchen.

However, even if you are not planning to install a new kitchen, still read on. You can slot many of the ideas shown on the following pages into your current layout. For example, you may be able to remove old, fixed shelves and insert new pull-out wire trays.

In properly designed kitchen storage there is a place for everything, within easy reach. The wall units of this stylish system have roller shutters, so that you can either hide all the equipment away or leave appliances on show.

KITCHEN STORAGE CHECKLIST

Before you buy special kitchen units and unit inserts to maximize your storage capacity, think about what you want to store, where you want to store it and how much space you need. Write a storage checklist and divide it into foods, pots, pans and crockery to be hidden, utensils and cutlery that you want to hand, items for display, rubbish to be recycled or thrown away, and cleaning materials.

❖ Canned and packet foods
❖ Fresh and frozen foods
❖ Pots, pans and utensils
❖ Electrical equipment
❖ Ovenware
❖ China and glassware
❖ Cutlery

❖ Tea and hand towels
❖ Table linen
❖ Plastic bags, foil and clingfilm
❖ Empty jars and bottles
❖ Rubbish bin
❖ Washing up materials
❖ Cleaning materials/equipment

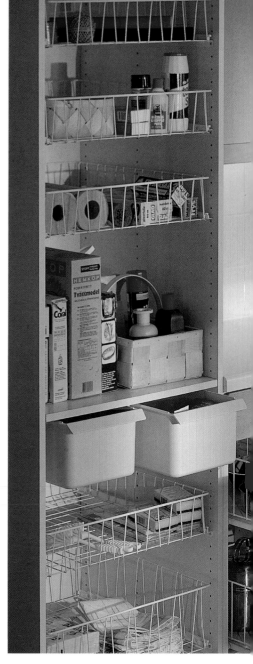

STORAGE ARRANGEMENTS

For greatest efficiency, organize storage round the three zones of the work triangle, as in the diagram below.

Food storage centres round the fridge, well out of the way of heat and steam. Use wall cupboards or open shelving for dry, packet goods such as flour, sugar and biscuits. If you choose open display, you can always decant the contents of the packets into attractive and clearly labelled storage jars. Store cans of food out of sight in floor-standing units, and vegetables and fruit in well-ventilated baskets.

Keep cleaning materials in a separate cupboard, as foodstuffs tend to pick up powerful smells. A tall cupboard is perfect for storing long brooms and mops. Store potentially toxic cleaning liquids on a high shelf, out of the reach of small children.

The food preparation area is next to the sink. Keep kitchen knives, strainers, graters, peelers and similar utensils in drawers immediately below the worktop, or hung from racks on the wall. Put china and crockery in open or concealed wall units, conveniently within reach of the washing up and serving areas between the sink and the cooker. A unit under the sink is the ideal place to keep a rubbish or recycling bin.

Small electrical appliances, such as a toaster, coffee maker, food mixer or blender, are best tucked out of the way along the back of a work surface or in drawers or pull-out units underneath. Don't store heavy items of equipment in wall units as they are awkward to lift up and down. For safety's sake, it's also most important to make sure that there is no chance of them falling into the sink.

In the cooking area you need deep drawers or double floorstanding cupboards for pots and pans, and baking sheets. Keep cooking utensils in shallow drawers or on a wall rack nearby. A special spice rack on the wall next to the cooker is both useful and attractive. A stack of drawers at the end of the worktop is the ideal place to store cutlery, table linen and tea towels.

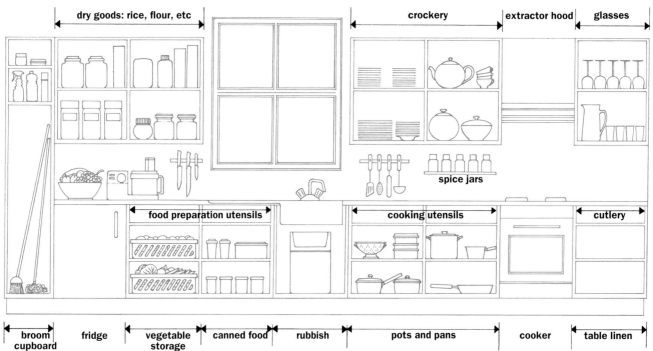

⬆ Everything in its place

A combination of tall units, wall units, deep, pull-out drawers and wire racks makes the best use of the available space in this small but efficient kitchen. Having plenty of room to store food, pots and pans, crockery and cleaning products helps to keep the worktops clear and tidy.

▶ Midway units

A neat shelf unit that fits between a wall unit and the worktop makes the most of an otherwise unused space and is invaluable for storing smaller items such as storage jars for tea or coffee, or pots of herbs and spices. A row of pegs underneath is handy for hanging mugs near the kettle or coffee maker.

THE STORAGE UNITS

Wall and base units are the backbone of most kitchen storage systems. They should incorporate a mixture of cupboards and drawers, both deep and narrow, to accommodate pots and pans as well as china, glassware and non-perishable food items.

WALL UNITS

Wall units must be a lot narrower than the worktop beneath, so you don't bang your head as you lean forward. Also avoid installing wall units over an empty space – you are likely to walk into them or catch yourself on sharp, head-height corners.

Most people can only reach the first and second shelves in their wall units, so use these to store everyday china and glass or frequently used cans and packet food. Store items that are used less frequently, like preserving jars for instance, on the higher shelves.

BASE UNITS

Kitchen base units house items of many different shapes and sizes, so it makes sense to have a combination of cupboards, drawers and open shelves of various heights.

Drawers Kitchen drawers are expensive, so think about how many you really need when planning your kitchen. You certainly need drawers for cutlery and for foldable items such as table linen and tea towels.

Pans, baking trays and casserole dishes are awkward to store because of their varying shapes and sizes. Wide, deep pan storage drawers designed to fit beside or beneath the oven or cooker top are a good idea. Check that the drawer is deep enough to hold your largest pan.

Shelves Save on the cost of base units by fitting wide shelves below a worktop. A curtain on a spring wire can hide things you don't want to display. You can use an open narrow infill space to store serving or baking trays.

Cupboards Carousels are designed to make every inch of space in wall and base units accessible. Although efficient at bringing items within easy reach, a carousel doesn't let you see everything on it all at once, as one side is always in the base unit.

◤ *Spice storage*
Jars of richly coloured spices and herbs look great hooked over a wall-fixed rod in a convenient position above the work surface.

◤ *Pan drawers*
Large pull-out drawers for pots and pans are essential. They allow you to store everything away neatly, near the oven. Indeed they can often be fitted underneath the cooker top itself.

◥ *Larder unit*
This unit is designed to store everything, however awkward the shape. Shallow shelves and racks fitted on the inside of the door make items even more accessible.

TALL UNITS

Luxury pantry cupboards are available custom-made from some kitchen manufacturers. Most have double doors, and are lined with wire or wicker shelves. The most expensive are fitted with a meat safe for cheese, hams and preserved sausages, and have a cooling unit in the base for beer and wine. A simpler, cheaper version is the tall pull-out larder unit, accessible from both sides and ideal for housing cans, bottles and packets.

MIDWAY UNITS

These compact shelf units are designed to make use of the space between worktop and wall units. Most manufacturers offer a range of midways. Narrow midway shelves are useful for herbs, spices and other frequently used ingredients. Small midway drawer units are good for keeping piping nozzles, petits fours tins and other small, easily mislaid bits and pieces.

OPEN SHELVING

Inexpensive, open shelving is a practical addition to both wall and base units, especially when you want to see or display the items in store. For extra flexibility, adjustable shelving allows you to change the structure of your storage system as your needs change.

☑ Simplifying saucepan storage
Slotting saucepan lids into a specially designed rack on the inside of a cupboard door frees the pans for easier stacking.

◪ Units plus shelves
With a combination of wall and drawer units plus midway and open shelving you really enjoy the best of all storage situations. You can display attractive bowls and ingredients you use regularly in your cooking on the shelves, while storing pots and pans out of sight behind the cupboard doors.

▶ Smaller-scale storage
This base storage unit does exactly what a larder unit does, but on a smaller scale. It is ideal for foods that you use often, like jams, tea, coffee, biscuits and certain canned foods.

CLEANING EQUIPMENT

Under the sink is the traditional spot for storing cleaning materials, but there is really only just enough room for the bare essentials. Use this space for washing up liquid, worktop cleaner and other cleansers in daily use. A custom-made storage rack that is designed to fit into under-sink cupboards makes the most of the limited space available.

You also need to find room for the vacuum cleaner, mop, broom, dustpan and brush, polish and shoe cleaning equipment. A tall cupboard with shelves top and bottom and enough space in-between for the taller cleaning accessories is ideal. Hooks on the underside of the top shelf and on the cupboard door are useful for hanging cleaning tools out of the way. The cupboard doesn't have to be in the kitchen, however. You might have more space in a utility room, garage, at the end of the hallway or under the stairs.

◤ *Under the sink*
In a kitchen, somewhere safe and inconspicuous to put rubbish is important. This carousel unit carries four separate containers for collecting different types of rubbish for the compost heap, the recycling bank or the refuse collection.

◂ *The cleaning cupboard*
A tall unit is really the only place to store brushes and mops in a kitchen. Fit it out with racks and shelves and you have one organized area in the kitchen that caters to all your cleaning needs.

◤ *Keeping items handy*
Cleaning utensils should be easy to reach. A pull-out rack means you don't need to scrabble around at the back of the cupboard for cleaning liquids, gloves and cloths.

REVAMPING A KITCHEN

*Take a good long look at your kitchen if it doesn't come
up to expectations. Maybe a quick lick of paint, or a few basic
changes, is all that's needed to give a new lease of life.*

D o you lack worktop space and storage, yet cannot justify a completely new kitchen? Are the fittings in your kitchen too good to discard, but not completely adequate? Is the kitchen layout workable, but the overall room dull and in need of a facelift?

It is quite possible to improve the look and efficiency of a kitchen for only a fraction of the cost of installing a new one, and with little disruption. First, take a long look at your kitchen to pinpoint the areas of dissatisfaction. Depending on your needs, a revamp can be anything from a quick cosmetic solution such as a lick of paint on jaded units to more drastic action, for example laying a new floor or extending existing cupboards.

To start you thinking, look through the checklists on the following pages which divide the work into major changes and quick revamps. If there's a lot of work to be done or your current budget won't stretch to a major overhaul, make long and short term plans.

A fresh coat of paint on wall and floor units and a bright display of china can make a kitchen lively and inviting.

PLANNING A REVAMP

Every kitchen is different, so solutions to problems posed by an unworkable layout or a dreary room will vary. Initial points to consider include the budget you need to set, and how long you plan to stay in your present home. A good kitchen is always a selling point, but you may not want to tackle anything too drastic if you're likely to move in a few years. Take into account the size of your family, and whether it may change – the arrival of a new baby or an elderly relative will affect how the kitchen is to be used.

To help you pinpoint areas of inefficiency, do your own time and motion study over a week or two. Are you constantly having to delve deep into low cupboards? Can you rehang a refrigerator door to save wasted steps? Ask family and friends for their views – often a fresh eye spots impracticalities you've got used to.

Adapting ideas for your own needs, work through the checklist below for major changes and look overleaf for quick solutions. Identify changes you can do yourself and any major tasks that need the help of a professional – arrange to have more than one estimate for structural changes: you'd be surprised at how much they can vary from one to another.

MAJOR PROBLEM SOLVERS

❖ **Is the kitchen cramped?** Make space by blocking up or diverting a door opening, or raising a low window, for extra wall or floor units. Rehang a door that blocks your path. Put the washing machine in a downstairs cloakroom or large walk-in cupboard if you have one. Extend the kitchen by opening up a wall into another room, to combine kitchen and dining activities.

❖ **Nowhere to put things?** Solve storage problems by adding shelves, or use wall grids or hanging racks for pots, pans and utensils. Fit custom-made wire storage trays in drawers and cupboards; make use of the backs of deep cupboards with slide-out drawers; fit carousels to corner cupboards.

❖ **Is the floor worn or impractical?** Two attractive floorcoverings that can be laid by a competent handyperson are wooden strip flooring or for a soft, warm option kitchen-grade washable carpet tiles.

❖ **Not enough space to work?** Release worktop space by wall-mounting the microwave and stowing small appliances such as a food processor in a slide-out drawer near a power point so they are ready for use. Extend work surfaces by adding a peninsula or island unit, if there's space.

❖ **Is the room dark and dreary?** Improve lighting with concentrated task lights, such as ceiling spotlights, for sink, cookers and preparation areas. Concealed strip lighting under shelves or cabinets helps light up dark areas and looks attractive at night. Let in plenty of natural light at the window with neat blinds or curtains draped back with tiebacks.

◧ *A neat and inexpensive solution to storage problems: new shelving painted to match kitchen cupboards is both functional and decorative.*

◧ *Well chosen new flooring completely transforms the look of a kitchen. A handsome border adds a stylish finishing touch to these black and white tiles.*

△ Touches of rich, bold colour, such as these sea-green tiles, give a kitchen character and warmth. To unify the effect, the same colour is used for walls and accessories.

◁ Opening out a room often gives a sense of space and lets extra light into a dark kitchen. Here a run of worktops and appliances has been added.

▷ Awkward spaces left by the removal of unwanted features can often be put to new use. Here, wall and floor cabinets are neatly housed in an alcove that once contained a redundant fireplace.

QUICK KITCHEN FACELIFTS

Simple changes involving little time or expense can make all the difference to a dreary kitchen. If the kitchen is workable but dull or the budget won't run to a major overhaul, check through the ideas below for cheerful finishing touches.

❖ **Freshen up walls** with a coat of paint or new wallcovering and a border – look for products specially made for a condensation-prone area. Add tiles to splashbacks and tile the wall between floor and wall units. To keep down costs, buy plain tiling and use a few more expensive decorated tiles as a border or pattern.

❖ **Give units a facelift** by painting old doors. If the finishes are in good condition but are drab, brighten them up with a stencilled motif or border, or pick out the mouldings in a different paint colour. Unit doorknobs and handles are cheap and easy to replace for a fresh look.

❖ **Add bright touches** by colour matching accessories such as storage jars, spice racks, tea towels, and other bits and pieces left on show.

❖ **Express individuality** with a collection of jugs on a shelf or dresser, coloured glasses or potted herbs at the window, or anything else that takes your fancy.

❖ **Add comfort** by slotting in a breakfast bar and stools, or a couple of chairs and a table – folding, pull-out or pull-down if space is tight.

▷ *A butcher's block trolley provides an extra work surface and additional storage space without the inflexibility of built-in fixtures.*

▲ *Imaginative touches here and there give real character to a kitchen. For a fair share of light the potted herbs on this ingenious shelf above the window are exchanged with those on the sill below.*

◀ *The window treatment in a kitchen, especially by a sink, is best kept simple – a crisp blind such as this is ideal.*

COUNTRY COTTAGE KITCHENS

Sunny, unpretentious and always inviting, you can interpret the cottage kitchen look in a totally traditional or more contemporary way, relying on natural materials with a handcrafted look to recreate its timeless appeal.

T he kitchen is the heart of the home in country living, a place where family and friends gather, assured of a warm reception and a welcoming drink, bite to eat or hearty meal. Recreating this feeling of old-fashioned, country-style hospitality in your own kitchen is simple, whether you actually live in the country or in an urban apartment, given the wide range of country-look storage units, furniture, fabrics and floor and wallcoverings available.

The look is based on practicality, with long-lasting, easy-to-clean surfaces and abundant storage space. A feeling of informality is important; cooking and other everyday chores can easily carry on regardless of who is in the room.

The country cottage style reflects the tradition of making furniture by hand and building houses from local materials, such as wood, bricks and tiles. Handcrafted pieces can be expensive, but luckily, modern manufacturing methods mean you can achieve a handcrafted look without paying a fortune and combine the convenience of the most up-to-date, state-of-the-art appliances with the lasting charm of the country-fresh style.

Quarry tile floors, exposed beams and simple pine furniture are hallmarks of the country-fresh kitchen, with flowers and greenery for added colour.

CREATING THE LOOK

Walls Solid white, cream or pale green painted or papered walls are just right for the look, especially as they help create a light-filled effect. Vertical tongue-and-groove boarding in similar colours is also fine. Old brick walls are charming, whether left in natural tones or painted white, although new bricks lack the same appeal.

Glazed tiles are practical but are best limited to small areas such as splashbacks for sinks or counters – lots of tiles, especially in white or pale colours, can create too modern and clinical a look. Alternatively, choose hand-painted tiles with floral motifs or simple geometric patterns.

Floors Hardwearing bricks are traditional, as are scrubbed or polished wooden floorboards, stone slabs and quarry tiles. Quarry tiles are the most authentic option if you are re-doing an existing kitchen. For a warmer, more comfortable alternative, choose modern vinyl, cork and other floorcoverings, some of which look convincingly like wood, stone, brick or quarry tiles.

Ceilings Wall colour and surface can continue over the ceiling for a unified look. In larger kitchens, make a contrast between wall and ceiling, for example by fixing tongue-and-groove boards to the ceiling of a plain, painted kitchen.

If you are lucky enough to have exposed beams in your kitchen, make the most of them by hanging bunches of dried flowers, or cooking utensils from hooks, S-shaped butchers' hooks or perhaps a laundry airer.

Lighting You can combine unobtrusive downlights set into the ceiling with more decorative, low-level pendant lighting over a dining table. You can light work surfaces with fluorescent strip lighting, hidden under wall units.

Window treatments If you have an urban outlook from you kitchen window, hang net curtains, or fix glass shelves across the window to hold leafy plants to obscure the view. Curtains range from simple café styles to more elaborate ruched blinds, and from solid tones and simple checks to spriggy floral patterns. Hang curtains on wooden rings from plain varnished wooden rods, or conceal the rods behind pine pelmets.

Finishes Simple tiled work surfaces are practical, heatproof and ideal for the look, especially if they continue on from nearby wall tiles. Plastic laminated worktops, in simulated wood or plain white are a practical, hardwearing and cheap alternative. But for the most authentic cottage-style work surfaces, you can't beat solid timber.

Fittings A true country kitchen needs an open range and a deep, old-fashioned ceramic butler's sink, with a traditional brass mixer tap and wooden draining boards, to set the scene perfectly. For an up-to-date approach, install an inset stone-look sink with an integrated drainer.

ELEMENTS OF THE STYLE

A thoroughly traditional version of the cottage look relies on plenty of timber, bricks, a butler's sink and an open range to set a cosy scene. Other pictures in this feature provide ideas for giving your kitchen a country-fresh look. Start with a few small touches, then build up the effect, adjusting the guidelines to suit your needs.

WALLS AND FLOOR

Go for solid white or pale, neutral walls, and easy-to-clean, hard-wearing floors. Make the most of exposed brick walls and/or open fireplaces, if you have them. Hang wood-framed, naïve-style animal or food theme prints or family photographs on the walls.

CEILING

A plain white ceiling keeps the room airy and bright. Wooden beams and rafters have a country feel and a decorative quality as well as being structural.

LIGHTING

An adjustable, counterbalanced, Victorian-style lamp provides a cosy light for dining, while brighter, more functional light comes from concealed strip lighting or downlights set into the ceiling.

STORAGE

Unmatched or coordinating stripped-pine, plain white or pale laminate storage units are ideal. A mixture of open cupboards, racks and shelves plus closed storage allows you to display your prettiest utensils and china, while concealing groceries. Old-fashioned storage containers of glass, china, pottery or tin set the style for little cost.

FURNITURE

Choose simple, rectangular or round stripped-pine tables and traditional ladderback or captains' chairs. Non-matching wooden chairs add a sense of fun.

WORK SURFACES

These are either tiled, solid wood or wood-effect laminate. Portable cutting boards and butchers' blocks are both practical and attractive.

KITCHEN FURNISHINGS

Tables and chairs A plain, stripped-pine table, whether new, secondhand or genuinely antique, is always right for the look, but one or two darker pieces in oak, for example, can look stunning. If you buy new furniture, choose solid pieces, rather than ornate styles. You can match or mismatch chairs, but always go for comfort – try them out first – with traditional styles , such as ladderback chairs, and solid or rush seats. Centring the table in the room is best, although you can push the table and chairs against one wall.

Storage Modular storage units in pine or white or pale laminate with simple knob handles are traditional, with a mixture of open and closed cup-

boards, and perhaps some fretwork detailing. If space allows, a big, old dresser, with open shelves for china and drawers for cutlery and kitchen linen, makes a good focal point for the room. You can create a dresser-like feel by adding parallel rows of wall shelving over an old chest of drawers.

Appliances If possible, store smaller appliances such as blenders and food processors behind cupboard doors, to provide more work space and maintain the illusion of timeless country living. You can hide larger modern appliances, which can look out of place in the country cottage theme, behind units with flush wooden doors to match or coordinate with kitchen cabinets.

◀ *Country bounty*

Oak shelves overflow with wicker baskets, some full of dried flowers, others left empty. Hanging bunches of dried flowers and a cheerful mix of china help to complete the cottage look.

◀ *Heart and home*

This country kitchen has an Aga to provide constant warmth and a butler's sink to cope with the washing up. A painted table, floral tiles and pretty stencilled curtain add to the cosy cottage feel.

▲ *Something old, something new*

Inexpensive modern pine furniture and kitchen units create a traditional country-style kitchen. The diamond-patterned floor, partly tiled walls and beamed ceiling provide an appropriate backdrop.

◀ *High-level charm*

Traditional blue and white china is displayed on a high shelf, with cream-painted, cast iron brackets adding an old-fashioned touch. Splashback tiles repeat the fresh blue and white theme.

To personalize your country cottage kitchen, display mixed china with old-fashioned patterns and wicker baskets filled with flowers or fruit, or a collection of baskets or jugs. Country produce of any sort, whether bunches of dried herbs, home-made preserves, vinegars or bread, is guaranteed to add to the look.

◄ Mix and match
Mixed blue and white china in traditional patterns, a wooden plate rack and an old-fashioned jug brimming with garden and hedgerow blooms add to the informal, easy-going style.

▲ Fruits of the vine
Simple, white stencilled vine motifs add a unifying touch to a traditional, glass-fronted pine dresser and pine and basketweave chairs.

◣ Well preserved
Pretty jars and bottles of preserves and vinegars with hand-written labels, gingham covers and bows make a very effective country kitchen display.

◄ Charming clutter
House plants and hand-made wooden toys look effective on a sunny windowsill. The boldly patterned tiles and shelves edged with lacy fretwork add interest and charm.

AMERICAN COUNTRY KITCHENS

Colourful, warm and welcoming, the American country-style kitchen has a simple, uncluttered look, economical to achieve and guaranteed to add freshness and individuality to your home.

The American country look, based on handcrafted, natural materials, functional style and simplicity, is a charming yet surprisingly sensible option, whether improving a kitchen or creating a new one. Like most country styles, its origins were firmly practical. The early settlers, far from European fashions and struggling to survive, lived without frills, relying on local material such as wood for building and furnishings.

Any decoration was equally basic and homespun. Flat patterns based on stylized fruits, flowers, animals, hearts, stars or geometric shapes were hand-painted, stencilled or carved; colours, ranging from muted to rich, came from the material itself or natural dyes.

Shaker style, named after an 18th century American religious sect whose austere, ultra-functional furniture and layouts have timeless appeal, can serve as inspiration, as can Pennsylvania Dutch ('Dutch' is a corruption of Deutsch, the settlers being German) style, with its more decorative emphasis on symmetrical, geometric patterns. But just by thoughtful choice of ordinary components and accessories you can achieve the warm feel of American country style, in a functional kitchen which forms the heart of the household.

This kitchen has a tidy, spacious feel, achieved through simple colour schemes and effective storage systems. Peg rails make use of the wall area, while baskets hung on runners make original vegetable racks.

81

CREATING THE LOOK

Walls Paint them white, cream, brick red, yellow ochre, teal blue, charcoal grey or dark green; or, for a light effect, combine white or pale walls with colourful woodwork: skirting boards, window frames and architraves.

Stencil simple borders at picture rail height or, if you're really keen, as an all-over motif. Alternatively, buy transparent stick-on stencil borders or stencil-patterned wallpaper, or striped, sprigged or simple geometric wallpapers. Pick up one of the colours in the woodwork, or paint one wall a solid colour.

Consider lining the walls, or at least the dado area, with matchboarding or tongue-and-groove panelling. You can either have it custom built or buy an easily assembled kit form to install yourself. The wood can be stained and varnished or colourwashed for a subtly aged effect.

Dutch-style blue and white tiles are another authentic wall covering; brick, left natural or whitewashed, can form whole walls or piers supporting work surfaces or a breakfast bar.

Floors Stone, clay tiles, brick paviors or wood, sanded and scrubbed, then oiled and waxed, are ideal; for economy and practicality, use top-quality vinyl look-alikes. If you have good floor-boards, stain, sand then seal them with a hard-wearing varnish, perhaps after stencilling a border or central 'rug'. For comfort underfoot and an authentic American look, add plain or checked fibre matting, or a colourful rag rug.

Windows Keep treatments unfussy: a roller blind or wooden Venetian blind is a neat solution; alternatively pin crocheted runners across the frame for privacy, or to block out an unattractive view.

When you'd rather hang curtains, stick to simple, sill-length ones in solid colours, bold calico prints, gingham checks, stripes, or stencilled or American-Indian type geometric patterns. You can stitch the curtains on to brass curtain rings, or have a half-height rod with café curtains. Coordinate tablecloths, place mats and tea towels with the curtain fabric for a pretty finishing touch.

Lighting Keep modern lighting fixtures unobtrusive. Candle-like fittings with white cotton or pleated shades suit the look much better. Candles in punched tin or wooden candle wall sconces in simple star or heart shapes, or a wrought iron or wooden candelabra hung over the kitchen table, add a period feel.

ELEMENTS OF THE STYLE

An orderly layout and natural materials typify the American country style; the key features are pinpointed here to inspire and help you to create a similar look in your kitchen. The pictures on the following pages show variations in the style and smaller decorative details that you can copy easily and inexpensively.

NATURAL MATERIALS

Wood is used extensively for cupboards, drawers and units, with modern appliances such as fridges and washing machines plumbed in behind, if possible.

STORAGE

Maximum use is made of wall and ceiling storage space. Kitchen utensils and light items of furniture – even small chairs – are hung high enough to be out of the way when not in use, but still remain accessible. In this way, humble household objects become decorative features as well. You can drill holes through wooden implements for easier hanging.

WALLS AND CEILINGS

These are painted in soft plain shades. Here, the cream colour contrasts well with the wooden beams. Walls can also be covered by wooden tongue-and-groove panelling.

LIGHTING

A graceful, genuine wooden candelabra lights up a kitchen table, although a candle-like electric fitting would create a similar effect.

ACCESSORIES

Classic Shaker storage boxes feature here, while simple craft decorations such as pottery, wicker and handmade doughcraft models add touches of detail.

FLOORS

Here, a stone floor is appropriately rustic, but quarry tiles, wood or vinyl look-alikes are suitable substitutes. All floors are kept clear.

KITCHEN FITTINGS

Storage Choose simple wooden cupboards and dressers, fitted or freestanding. Follow the Shaker principle of 'a place for everything and everything in its place', by having cupboards with different sized shelves and drawers for various sizes of china, glass and cutlery, or freestanding, all-in-one units, combining drawers and cupboards. Choose old or new pine, which you can stain and varnish yourself, if you wish, or paint or colourwash in soft, dusky shades, then stencil with folk images.

Shelves with fretwork or scalloped edges and wrought iron hinges and handles to cupboard doors are suitable and attractive options. Marble, slate and wooden work surfaces are traditional, but good-quality simulated alternatives are more reasonably priced and practical.

Ornate but solidly built furniture such as a polished dark wood dresser is also suitable, since the more affluent American settlers initially brought these items with them from Europe, and later imported them or bought American-made versions. You can buy good-quality dark wood pieces second hand, by hunting them out in junk shops and auctions.

If you have enough space, use a painted pine blanket box to provide additional storage. Then you can create extra seating by making a check or patchwork squab cushion to fit on the top.

Appliances Brightly enamelled cast-iron stoves, fitted with shiny brass trivets, pot-hooks and rails, are customary, as are inviting open fireplaces. Modern appliances and labour-saving devices can be concealed behind wooden units or displayed in honest contrast to their period surroundings.

Tables and chairs Choose sturdy, practical furniture. Self-descriptive ladderback chairs, with cane, rush or woven tape seats, and simple trestle or refectory-style tables are ideal; in a confined space, choose a drop-leaf table, and fold the sides away when not in use. Slightly more ornate furniture might feature barley-sugar twisted legs. If space permits, include a comfortable wooden rocking chair, complete with patchwork cushion for a genuine, early-American image.

▶ *Tidy storage*
A hanging rail is an alternative to the Sha[k] peg rail, while the sturdy streamlined cupboard can be used [to] store kitchen utensils.

◀ *The kitchen table*
Old rustic chairs and table in natural wood are set off by the soft blue and green painted walls. The quilted patchwork tablecloth and wooden candle sconce help to create authentic American country character.

Spotlights provide
unobtrusive lighting for work
surfaces and the cooking area
while the wrought iron
candelabra provides light and
a focal point for a sturdy table
and Shaker-influenced
slatback chairs. A decorative
collection of well used copper
pots and pans is stored out of
the way on a ceiling rack.

◥ *Natural materials*

Here, decorative wicker baskets
are hung from a rafter. The tiles
along the back wall have an
appealing folk design and the
shiny texture of the tiled surface
contrasts well with the
surrounding matt wooden
surfaces and units. The simple
table and chairs continue the
natural wood theme.

85

Anything with a handmade quality is ideal for enhancing this country style. Use framed samplers, embroidery and naive pictures, or country prints in stencilled frames, to create focal points on walls, and carved wooden animal ornaments on window sills or mantelpieces.

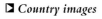

▶ Country images
Natural pine furniture can be painted in muted tones; the panels of this cupboard feature 'folk-art' animal cards, cut to fit.

◀ Handcrafted charm
Handpainted or stencilled motifs, in subtle colours, summon up a handcrafted country style.

◥ Shaker style
Hang attractive utensils on a peg by leather thongs or coloured cord.

APARTMENT KITCHENS

Fresh-looking and stylish on a shoestring budget, with a functional, orderly approach to make maximum use of compact space, the apartment kitchen is a delight to work and dine in.

M ore dash than cash is the theme of the modern apartment kitchen, with its sleek, glossy look based on light, bright, airy colour schemes, flush surfaces and attention to even the most minute detail. Though space is at a premium, work, storage, cooking and dining areas are very convenient and comfortable; cupboards, appliances and units form clean, smooth-flowing lines and inventive storage arrangements keep utensils and china neat but handy. Especially decorative pieces can double as ornaments. Plenty of white creates an illusion of space, while practical window treatments, such as plain blinds, and compact, functional furniture create a streamlined, unfussy feel.

If you are starting from scratch, you are spoilt for choice by the newest ranges of materials and appliances on the market. However, if you're cheering up an existing kitchen, you needn't spend a lot of money. Study the following pages for inspiration and clever ideas.

A light, fresh colour scheme makes a narrow kitchen seem spacious, while streamlined fitted units conceal kitchen equipment, cleaning materials and appliances.

CREATING THE LOOK

Walls Go for white or bright solid or boldly striped colours with a matt finish – dark colours overpower a small space. To make the room seem larger, match wall colour to worktops and units, perhaps with details picked out in contrasting colours. Tile or retile walls behind a worktop in plain tiles. Tile over old ones, and rejuvenate dull tiles with coloured grout.

Window treatments Choose neat, tidy roller or Venetian blinds – a London blind or curtains would be too fussy. Use blinds to introduce bright solid colour or a striped or geometric pattern. Louvred shutters make a striking feature, while letting light in and hiding an ugly view at the same time.

Flooring Choose tough, easy-to-clean flooring. Sheet lino and vinyl are inexpensive, comfortable and come in many colours. Black and white geometric patterns or traditional tile-patterned vinyls look good. Alternatively, go for pale wood, sealed for easy cleaning, or quarry or ceramic tiles; ceramic tiles come in many styles – they are costly, but you don't need many in a small space.

Lighting Wall- and ceiling-mounted spotlights concentrate light where it is needed most. Choose discreet task lighting over worktops – hide strip lighting beneath wall units. Subtle lighting in glass-fronted cupboards shows off the contents. A flexible downlighter over the table provides general light when raised, an intimate pool of light when lowered.

Finishes Plastic laminated worktops are hardwearing, inexpensive and sold in a variety of styles, from pastel and primary colours to simulated wood, granite and marble. White laminated worktops and units look fresh and go with anything. Laminated worktops come in high gloss and more scratch-resistant matt finishes. To replace existing worktops, buy laminated boards in cut lengths from DIY or home centre shops. Plain tiles are easy to clean and heatproof. Real marble, granite or slate or convincing reproductions add a touch of opulence and are virtually indestructible, but they are expensive.

ELEMENTS OF THE LOOK

A simple, strong colour scheme, streamlined fittings and an overall functional approach typify the modern apartment kitchen. Note the key features pinpointed here when creating the look in your own kitchen.

WALLS AND CEILING

These are painted white or in solid matt colours for a simple, airy feel. Light wood trimmings on units add a natural touch; bright, primary trim would be equally attractive. Tiles behind the work surfaces are clean-looking and hygienic.

FLOORING

Tough vinyl flooring is practical and unfussy. Here, a 'sea' of rich blue provides a strong contrast to the walls and units, and the slight speckle pattern helps conceal the marks of daily wear and tear.

STORAGE

Drawers, cupboards, open shelves and a hanging rail provide ample storage for utensils, crockery and food. A central, circular hanging rail above the table would make an attractive, space-saving feature.

LIGHTING

Built-in spotlights above work surfaces provide discreet task lighting, without casting a harsh glare over the room or creating visual clutter. A hanging downlighter over the table provides intimate light for dining.

WINDOW TREATMENTS

A striped blind introduces strong pattern, combines the blue and white of the colour scheme and, when rolled up, takes minimal space and light from the window. Curtains, ruching and fussy blinds are definitely out.

APPLIANCES

The fridge freezer and washing machine are concealed behind fitted unit doors, preserving a uniform appearance and flush surface. The oven is a discreet, modern slide-in model with an extractor fan above to eliminate cooking smells.

FURNITURE

The small table doubles as a work surface. Director's chairs can be folded and put away to create space, if needed. Folding side tables and countertop tables with stools are sensible options in very compact kitchens.

KITCHEN FITTINGS

Storage Keep china dust free in glass-fronted units. For a similar light, but more casual look, open shelving is cheaper and the contents more accessible. Pull-out cupboards with wire shelves and removable storage baskets are perfect. Fill high-level corners with plain shelves or corner cupboards with revolving carousel shelves. Use narrow spaces as tidy compartments for trays or wine bottles.

Appliances Select a stainless steel or white ceramic sink, with a waste disposal unit if possible. Conceal fridges, freezers and dishwashers behind unit doors. Slim-line washing machines save space. Choose compact slide-in cookers that match units at plinth and worktop level.

Tables and chairs Small folding tables can be wall hung, or dropsided types pushed against a wall for daily use and pulled out and expanded for parties. A large kitchen table is great, if space allows.

If cupboards leave no room for stools or knees, the ultimate space-saver is a pull-out eating surface. When closed, these tabletops look like drawers; when open they can seat one or two people. Some have legs attached and can double as work surfaces. You might prefer a purpose-built counter – attached to the wall by hinges and folded down when not in use.

Use wooden or chrome twist-up bar stools, or buy director's chairs or smart tubular steel framed chairs with wicker seats to go with the kitchen table.

◢ *Painting unit doors*

If you can't replace unit doors, paint them instead. Clean the surface with methylated spirits (denatured alcohol), wash with detergent, dry, then roughen it by rubbing with wetted wet and dry paper. You don't need to apply primer or undercoat; just use two coats of satin finish paint and thin the first one slightly.

◢ *Checkmate*

Bold black and white chequerboard flooring introduces strong contrast, geometric pattern and a touch of the traditional into an otherwise pale scheme. Twist-up stools are ideal for countertop dining – here one side of the countertop doubles as a display shelf.

◤ *Wall to wall*

A fitted unit and glass-fronted cupboards revealing their orderly contents fill the end wall of this narrow kitchen, leaving space for a table, bench and fold-away chairs. Natural wood furniture, splashback, and door handles add a unified touch.

◀ *White on white*

Perfectly flush, vertical and horizontal surfaces of solid, dazzling white create an illusion of space in a very small, galley-type kitchen. A tiny polka dot pattern on the wall tiles adds a cheerful touch, and central ceiling spotlights provide light without clutter.

◤ *City slicker*

Hard, reflective materials such as marble, chrome and stainless steel create an ultra-stylish, up-to-date look, while angled, fitted units make use of every bit of available space.

DETAILS

You can replace your standard kitchen unit doors with new ones or remove them to make open shelf units. Increase storage space by fitting wire wall grids, or a curtain pole or plumber's copper piping to the wall. For a quick change, add coordinated storage jars, spice racks, paper towel holders, tea towels and oven gloves, or leafy house plants, and display framed posters on walls.

◭ Hanging around

Hanging rails keep essential utensils within easy reach.

◭ Spicing up the look

Shiny stainless steel canisters are a slick, stylish alternative to glass or ceramic jars. Lightweight and unbreakable, with close fitting lids, they're ideal for storing pungent herbs and spices.

◭ Artistic touch

Hand-painted ceramic jars in bold, bright colours are a lively addition to any kitchen.

◭ Wired up

Wire storage baskets come in a huge range of styles and sizes. Their metallic look complements smooth, sleek finishes.

▸ Smart as paint

Inexpensive open shelving is painted a stylish bright blue to provide a perfect showcase for kitchen crockery and utensils. The other woodwork is painted in an identical blue colour, to bring customized style to the room.

MEDITERRANEAN KITCHENS

For practicality, informality and rustic good looks, choose the sun-drenched, flamboyant colours, natural materials and hand-crafted finishes of a Mediterranean-style kitchen.

P reparation of food in the Mediterranean way of life is a labour of love; and family meals, however modest, are an unhurried and enjoyable social event. Mediterranean kitchens, with their bowls of fresh fruits and vegetables, bunches of dried herbs, bottles of aromatic oils and well worn cooking utensils proudly on display, reflect this love of food in all its forms.

The Mediterranean kitchen is solid, practical and down to earth, with rustic, rural or seaside overtones. Though stone or tiled floors, rough plastered walls and heavy wooden beams are traditional, you can give an ordinary kitchen a Mediterranean look with simple wooden furniture and well chosen accessories such as hand-painted china, rustic glassware, ceramic

storage containers and Provençal-style table cloths, napkins and curtains.

Colour is very important, with bright royal blue, saffron yellow, brick red, olive green and dusky pink predominant, often in typical Provençal mini-print patterns, against a backdrop of colour-washed or fresh white walls.

A large dining table often forms the kitchen's focal point, emphasizing that cooking and dining are seen as a continuous process. With this layout, the family cook is still part of the ongoing conversation as he or she makes those essential, last-minute adjustments – a pinch of seasoning, a sprinkle of fresh herbs or parmesan cheese – that are so much a part of Mediterranean cuisine.

Small touches, such as charming, Provençal-style fabrics, dried herbs, a fruit-filled basket and a big jar of olives can give an ordinary modern kitchen a sunny, Mediterranean feel.

CREATING THE LOOK

Walls Rough plastered stone walls are traditional, but you can paint plain walls white or create a weathered, textured look with colour washes in bold or soft, muted tones, using emulsion or vinyl matt paint. Or, for an instant colourwashed effect, use one of the washable wallpapers printed to give the same look and now readily available. Combine white or pale, plain or colourwashed walls with woodwork painted in rich Mediterranean hues.

Use plain, mini-print or hand-painted glazed tiles, vertically or diagonally, for splashbacks behind the sink, cooker and work surfaces. Easier to clean than paintwork or wallpaper, the tiles can also complement hand-painted pottery and Provençal fabrics. If funds allow, consider fully tiling the lower half of the walls.

Floors Natural stone slabs, stripped wood or terracotta tiles, plain or with a contrasting tile trim border, are authentic. Good quality vinyl floorcovering in simulated terracotta, wood or stone, and large chequerboard patterns, in black and white or colours toning with the decor, are reasonably priced alternatives.

Windows Wooden louvred shutters are perfect for a sunny window; internal shutters, left permanently open, create the feeling of a sunny atmosphere, whatever the natural light. For privacy or to conceal a dull outlook, choose pale-coloured or plain white Roman blinds, slatted blinds, simple muslin sill-length curtains, Provençal-style café curtains or lace panels hung from brass rods.

Lighting A drop light with a simple metal shade and positioned centrally over the dining table is typical. For practicality, fit strip lighting over work surfaces but make sure it is fully concealed. For a decorative effect, display candles in wrought-iron wall sconces or free-standing, table-top candlesticks.

ELEMENTS OF THE STYLE

This contemporary kitchen, with its natural materials, sunny colours and layout based round a central dining table, typifies the Mediterranean style. Use some or all of the elements shown here and on the following pages as inspiration to help you create a similar look in your own kitchen.

WINDOWS

A simple, shaped roller blind, mini-windowbox – ideal for growing culinary herbs – and a hint of external iron grillwork allow as much light into the room as possible.

ACCESSORIES

Storage jars and bottles, ropes of onions, a wooden chopping board and plate rack and a set of scales all give the impression of a working kitchen. Chunky, sprigged crockery, including a generously filled fruit bowl, adds a burst of colour.

SOFT FURNISHINGS

Squab cushions, table linen and a window blind in busy, mix-and-match patterns – Indian paisley, mini-sprigs, stylized flowers and leaves – create an authentic Mediterranean feel and add vigour to the room.

FLOORS

Large, square terracotta floor tiles are typically Mediterranean. Alternatively, you can use a good quality, look-alike vinyl floorcovering or keep to bare wooden boards.

WALLS

Fresh white and blue tiles form a continuous splashback between work surfaces and wall-mounted cupboards, for a practical wallcovering with plenty of style.

FURNITURE

A sturdy wooden table with a scrubbed pine surface, and sides and legs painted blue to match the ladderback chairs, forms the focal point of the room. Fitted kitchen units, painted fresh white with blue detailing, are an updated version of the look and provide plenty of storage.

FITTINGS AND FURNITURE

Storage Huge armoires or stately wooden cabinets with decoratively curved and carved fronts, are traditional features in Mediterranean kitchens. They often formed part of a bride's dowry and were handed down from one generation to the next. Solid, rustic wooden dressers, shelves and cupboards, combining simple straight lines and gentle curves, are authentic alternatives – even the smallest kitchen can accommodate a corner cupboard. Walnut is the preferred wood, but cherry, pear, olive, chestnut and scrubbed or stained pine are fine.

Eye-level open storage for display is generally best, with low-level closed storage for more mundane items. In a contemporary kitchen, simple white or two-toned wood or wood-finish fitted storage units blend well with the look. Choose marble, slate, wood or tiled work surfaces, if funds allow, or authentic reproductions.

Appliances Free-standing cookers and sinks are traditional, but built-in appliances are a practical alternative, especially in compact fitted kitchens. The appliances can be concealed or on show, in which case white is the traditional, timeless choice of colour.

Table and chairs Continuing the wood theme, a sturdy wooden table which can double as a work surface when it is not being used for dining is almost essential. Give it pride-of-place in the centre of the room.

Surround the table with high-backed wooden chairs – ideally they should have rush or cane seats for the right rustic look, ladder-backed types are ideal. Alternatively, plain wooden chairs with solid seats and squab cushions for comfort are just as appropriate. The chairs needn't necessarily match the table or each other – in fact, a mixture of woods from rich to pale is in keeping with the informal mood of the room. Or, paint the mismatched chairs the same strong, cheerful colour.

Pretty, hand-painted detailing on wooden chairs and kitchen cupboards is typical; popular motifs include turtle doves, hearts, vine leaves, grapes and flowers.

◘ *Indoor scents*

Capture the fragrance of the Mediterranean with terracotta flower pots of rosemary, as shown, or thyme or sage, placed on a sunny windowsill. Use them as a centrepiece for a table set with Provençal napkins and bread-filled wicker baskets.

◢ Rustic influence

Colourwashed walls and
rustic furniture create relaxed
kitchen decor. The corner
cupboard doors, hung with
lavender and garlic are left
open to reveal a medley of
crockery, spices and table
linen. The other cupboard
echoes the first but with a
twist – the wired doors reveal
a trompe l'oeil display.

◣ Artistic touch

A love of decorative detail is
evident in the Mediterranean
home, with hand-painted
wooden furniture one of the
key examples. Here, a chair
and tray become works of art
with saffron yellow stencils.

◢ Well integrated

A wall of continuous, low-level
units, set in matching tile
surrounds, maximizes storage space
and provides plenty of surfaces for
preparing food and displaying
bright crockery. The ladderback,
rush-seated chairs, flowers and
house plants add a personal touch.

◣ Clever camouflage

Large appliances such as a
double oven can be discretely
fitted into understated
storage units. In a modern
kitchen like this, capture the
Mediterranean theme with
accessories – pots and herbs
displayed from a ceiling-
hung rack, framed prints
and fresh sunflowers.

The Mediterranean kitchen is a working kitchen, so the more utensils, crockery and raw ingredients on display, the better! Go for hand-painted dishes in colourful or earthy tones, and use Provençal fabrics for everything from curtains to bread-basket liners as a lively, unifying touch.

▶ Fresh primaries
Turk's-cap ranunculus, hand-painted pottery and rustic, tinted glassware enhance the mix-and-match, blue, yellow and red patterned table linen.

◀ Earthy option
A collection of chunky, hand-painted, glazed stoneware and terracotta bowls and jugs in earthy tones epitomizes the functional yet stylish nature of the Mediterranean look.

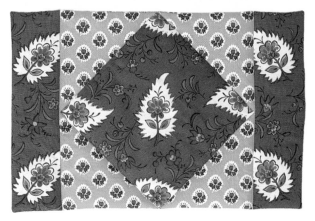

◀ Provençal patchwork
Simple geometric patchworks in toning, bold and mini-print Provençal fabrics make ideal placemats, table cloths and napkins.

▲ Perfect packaging
Keep attractively bottled French condiments, such as cooking oils and vinegars, on display.

Soft Modern Kitchens

Preparing and eating meals is a pleasure in the relaxed, comfortable and spacious setting of the soft modern kitchen, with its emphasis on natural materials, clean lines and neutral tones.

S implicity is the key to this light, airy style, with smooth, sleek lines and fittings enlivened by cheery personal touches – a wickerwork basket of rosy red apples on the work surface, a vase of fresh flowers brightening up the breakfast bar, natural cotton tea towels and oven gloves hanging from a neat row of pegs behind the door. Any design statement in the soft modern kitchen is quiet rather than strident, and though basically modern, the look is not coldly clinical nor does it depend on the latest, easily outdated fad. Feel free to mix elements from various styles and periods, as long as you combine them thoughtfully.

Use pale, neutral tones, ranging from white to ivory, cream, beige and dove grey, to create a light and airy backdrop, to which you can give a crisp, modern edge with contrasting flashes of stainless steel or warm up with mellow-toned light wood and wickerwork accessories. Bold accent colours tend to be small-scale and transient, rather than part of the permanent decor, to keep colour options open – the soft modern look is nothing if not adaptable. Natural or natural-look materials are the order of the day, and practicality precludes any surface difficult to clean, as well as any fussy or ornate detail.

Though you can achieve the look in any reasonably sized kitchen, those without elaborate, built-in period architectural detail, such as ornate cornices, are especially suitable. Collect and compare paint, fabric and surface material samples before choosing a narrowly harmonious colour theme; some manufacturers offer colour and pattern coordinated ranges of paints, washable wallpapers and fabrics, but you can be more adventurous, mixing and matching from several sources.

The eminently practical soft modern kitchen is based on simple fitted units, clean lines, natural materials and neutral tones. Handsomely designed utensils and decorative objects, like the woven basket, bold ceramics, jug of fresh flowers and bowls of fruit shown here, add a colourful, personal touch.

ACHIEVING THE STYLE

Walls and ceilings For a generously roomy effect, choose white or pale solid tones. You can paint, paper or tile the walls – glazed tiles are especially practical behind work surfaces. Reproduction, faux marble panels are equally practical for horizontal work surfaces and adjacent splashbacks, and their cool tones perfectly reflect the look. Alternatively, cover walls and possibly the ceiling with sealed, natural stripped pine, tongue and groove boarding, laid either vertically or horizontally; if it matches pine or pine-effect fitted units, so much the better. You can treat walls and ceilings separately, but go for a soft rather than jarring contrast.

Floors Flooring should echo the mellow tones and natural theme of the other surfaces. Choose easy-to-wash stripped or stained pine, or opt for inexpensive and hardwearing linoleum or vinyl flooring with a pine-effect finish, or in a pale neutral shade or speckled mini-print design. Terracotta or quarry tiles, or tile-effect vinyl, are other options.

Window treatments Keep these simple, though you can discreetly highlight the window by painting the frame, mullions and sill a contrasting crisp white or softly neutral colour, such as blue-grey, perhaps repeating the treatment on architraves and skirting boards. Fitted Venetian blinds give a sharp, modern edge, while woven cane blinds or fabric roller blinds in plain or bold, modern patterns have a slightly more relaxed feel. If you wish, soften the effect with sill-length, sheer or lightweight unlined curtains. Natural, lightly textured fabrics work best.

Lighting Make the most of natural light and keep artificial lighting adaptable. Concealed strip lighting above work surfaces is practical and space-saving and can also be used to illuminate display shelves. Fix an adjustable-drop, pendent light with a simple frosted glass or stainless steel shade over a dining table – or a row of them over a breakfast bar – to isolate these areas from the hubbub of the main kitchen and create an intimate atmosphere at cosy family meals. For a more discreet alternative, use recessed downlighters built into the ceiling; a series of small, high-tech pendants fitted with spotlight bulbs would tilt the look in a truly modern direction.

ELEMENTS OF THE LOOK

The soft modern kitchen is easy to use and has a welcoming, relaxed feel, without compromising on style. Here the key features of the look are picked out to help you recreate it in your own home, and variations on the style are given on the following pages.

WINDOWS

A wood-weave roller blind gives privacy while filtering rather than completely blocking out the light. The effect is softened with floaty, sill-length sheer curtains in a dainty self-check, hung from a pale beech curtain pole.

ACCENTS

Gleaming metal accessories – including a wirework basket, stainless steel kettle, chrome toaster and a novel star-shaped wine-rack – add flashes of modernism, while natural wood and wickerwork, in the form of a wall-mounted plate rack, a chopping board, basket and tray, strike a more mellow note.

TABLE AND CHAIRS

A glass and beech table, teamed with three woven cane and one polished wood chair, are natural choices. The glass-topped table takes up little visual space, so is a good choice for small rooms and airy schemes.

LIGHTING

A simple, central pendent ceiling light with a steel and frosted glass shade illuminates the table. Add concealed strip lighting over work surfaces for maximum visibility when you're preparing food.

STORAGE

White fitted units look sleek and streamlined; dainty rounded handles and moulded detailing give them added interest and character. The low-level units with solid doors conceal mundane items and large appliances; glass-fronted, eye-level units double as display cabinets, containing more decorative crockery and glassware.

WALLS AND FLOOR

Tongue-and-groove boarding, colourwashed in the same fresh yellow as the walls then varnished for protection, makes a stylish and original splashback with a homely feel. Pale woodstrip flooring follows through the natural theme and is a practical choice.

SOFT MODERN FURNISHINGS

Storage Wall-to-wall fitted units are ideal for the look, providing plenty of space for hiding away unattractive clutter and giving a neat, streamlined finish. These needn't break the bank – by shopping wisely at DIY outlets and specialized kitchen showrooms, you can often take advantage of seasonal sales or special promotional offers; and if you are keen on DIY, this too can keep costs down.

Choose low- and high-level fitted storage units, with a good mixture of drawers and fixed and adjustable shelves. Laminated plastic, wood or wood-effect laminate surfaces forming a continuous, smooth, flush finish, and simple knob or D-handles, add to the sleek look. Decorative panelling or fretwork can be incorporated, as long as it's restrained. Open or glass-fronted cupboards allow ornamental kitchenware, china and utensils to become part of the display, as well as helping to open out the room. For storing less decorative items, you could opt for high-level cupboards with frosted or patterned glass fronts, then fit them with internal strip lights to give bright panels of pleasantly diffuse light.

If space allows, fit wooden hanging rails for storing utensils, tea towels or other small items, and complete your storage options with very simple glass, ceramic or stainless steel canisters.

Appliances Modern appliances of a simple design add to, rather than detract from, the look, so feel free to keep them on display. Try to incorporate them in amongst the fitted units to minimize wasted space and tricky-to-clean corners. Eye-level microwave ovens, for example, can fit neatly into housing units or below wall-mounted cupboards, and sleek, stainless steel cooker tops and sinks set into work surfaces all add to the room's streamlined feel.

A place to eat Though smart and stylish, the soft modern kitchen is also a relaxed, pleasant environment where you can enjoy family meals and informal suppers with friends; so if space allows, include a sturdy table, or breakfast bar, and comfortable chairs – strictly speaking, cushions are not part of the look, so test seating carefully for comfort before buying. Unlike the fitted units, which are basically right-angled and neutral, your table and chairs can express a more personal, even period style and incorporate flowing, sinuous curves as well as right angles. They can be of the same or contrasting materials and colours, but keep to neutral shades and natural materials so they blend with the look. A glass-topped table is a good idea in small kitchens as it takes up little visual space.

◀ *Clean lines*
Matt, white laminate kitchen units and glossy granite-effect work surfaces, set against a backdrop of bright blue tiled walls, give this kitchen a streamlined, fresh and airy feel. A pale woodstrip floor adds a welcome warm note.

▶ *Soft and modern*
This elegant kitchen strikes a perfect balance between the soft, mellow tones of natural wood – in the overhead storage cupboard and the unit fronts – and the hard, industrial gleam of metal on the stainless steel work surfaces, hob and cooker. A vase of sculptural arum lilies and a bowl of lemons add fresh, tangy accents.

◀ Natural appeal

It's the use of natural materials that lifts the hard edge off the soft modern kitchen and gives it its warmth and character. Here, beech veneer units and an oiled beech breakfast bar are set against a backdrop of rough brick walls, a brick floor and a wooden board ceiling. Steel chairs, slate-coloured worktops and high-tech lighting give a modern slant, while cooking ingredients on the worktop show this is a lived-in kitchen.

▶ Go with the flow

This smooth, continuous frontage of fitted storage units contains closed cupboards for mundane items and open cupboards for storing cook books and decorative pottery. Dark wood worktops and flooring and pale blue paintwork at the window provide visual relief from the smooth-flowing colour of the units and walls.

◣ Kitchen essentials

Natural cotton tea towels and oven gloves – either plain or in simple two-colour checks – are perfectly in keeping with the simple, smart yet friendly feel of the soft modern kitchen.

Balance the cool geometry of kitchen fittings with handcrafted objects, such as terracotta pottery, and the organic shapes of fresh flowers, pots of herbs and colourful fruit. And look to glinting metals to add a modern edge to mellow backgrounds.

▶ Streamlined storage
Top-hinged, glass-fronted overhead cupboards with a continuous shelf running beneath them are a sleek, easy-access solution to storage problems. Cupboards with obscured or transparent glass fronts give an airier impression than opaque alternatives.

◀ A glint in your eye
Look to modern-style, metallic accessories to enliven a neutral backdrop and bring a scheme right up to date.

▲ All that glitters
A handy display of stainless steel or aluminium containers and utensils continues the theme of streamlined surfaces, adds a reflective accent and – most importantly – aids in the preparation of food.

◀ An apple a day
Seasonal fruits in a traditional wooden lath basket provide cheap, instant and easily renewable colour. Real or realistic or stylized painted wooden fruit can do the job equally well.

KITCHEN STORAGE JARS

*Tidy ingredients away and keep them fresh in kitchen
storage jars and tins – they also create an attractive display
on shelves, table tops and work surfaces.*

S torage jars are essential in any organized kitchen – especially if you have open shelving rather than cupboards. The jars look much more attractive than having an untidy mix of half-full packets and bottles scattered about the place. And if you choose well-sealed, airtight jars, like preserving jars, they'll keep the food fresh for longer too.

There is a huge range of storage jars available, so it's simply a case of finding a style that appeals to you and suits the decor of your kitchen. You can buy a smart matching set of

jars, or put together an interesting, mixed collection. Glass jars are a stylish, inexpensive option, and allow you to see their contents at glance. There are ceramic jars to suit all tastes and budgets as well. Choose ones that are labelled for ease of use, or label them yourself.

Be sure to buy a mixture of jar sizes to accommodate different ingredients – small jars for seasonings and spices, medium-sized jars for sugar, flour, tea, coffee and so on, and large jars for foods like pasta and pulses which take up a surprisingly large amount of space.

White ceramic tea caddies make elegant kitchen storage jars. Teamed with blue and white crockery they create a handsome display on the shelves of this dresser.

▶ **Glass storage jars** allow you to see at a glance where your cooking ingredients are. They're stylish, inexpensive and give the kitchen a workaday feel.

▼ **Keep food fresh** in airtight preserving jars, available in a range of attractive styles.

◀ **Summer fruits** painted on to these ceramic jars are a fresh motif for the kitchen – follow through with fruit-themed teatowels and oven gloves.

▲ **Make an impact** with bright, rainbow-striped storage jars, guaranteed to brighten up the dullest kitchen corner. Try painting your own cheerful designs using special ceramic paints; paint the outside of the jar and lid only.

▶ **Keep an eye open for old tins** and jars like these – they make delightful storage containers for country-style kitchens. Plenty of clearly labelled storage jars of all descriptions – all facing forwards for instant ease of recognition – are the key to an orderly and handy display of ingredients.

THE HERB KITCHEN

Growing herbs in your kitchen not only means that you have a ready supply at hand to use in your cooking, but the scented greenery also pervades your home with a delightful touch of freshness.

Herbs are grown for a number of reasons – for adding flavour to food, for their medicinal properties or simply for their scents. Growing your own herbs is easy – many big supermarkets now sell pots of fresh herbs that you can replant or you can grow them yourself from seed. Position herbs on a sunny windowsill or shelf in your kitchen, water them regularly and they should thrive quite happily. Growing herbs indoors means that they are protected from frost so that you can choose more delicate varieties.

Although the main attractions of the herbs are their green, fragrant leaves, most herbs also produce small, delicate flowers in the summer. Chives, marjoram and thyme, for example, all produce pink or purple flowers, while rosemary produces pale blue flowers.

Small terracotta pots or troughs make attractive containers for herbs on windowsills, but if you haven't got space by the window, think about putting up some shelves and making the herbs an eye-catching feature of the kitchen. Make sure you choose a wall that gets plenty of light, as most herbs need a well-lit position to do well. When choosing herbs, try to select leaves of different shapes and sizes in varying shades of green to create an attractive display.

You may like to dry some of your harvest of fresh herbs to make pot pourri for scenting your linen or to use in your cooking later on. Hang bunches of the freshly picked herbs, leaves downwards, on a wall or suspended from the ceiling, to add an aromatic country cottage touch to your kitchen.

Herbs growing in terracotta troughs make an attractive display in this light, airy kitchen. Sitting on especially erected shelves like this means the herbs are handy for picking as you need them when cooking.

◪ Corner shelves with holes for herb containers are a clever space-saving idea and allow the coloured pottery containers to be shown to advantage. It is the perfect place for a welcome touch of greenery in this small kitchen.

▶ Bunches of fresh herbs hanging up to dry add a rustic touch to any kitchen. The pretty pink and purple flowers of sage, marjoram and thyme blend delicately with the soft greens of the herbal leaves.

◪ Bright little bags of home-dried herbs, tied at the necks with scarlet ribbon and identified by a nosegay of the appropriate herb, look charming on a dresser shelf and would make delightful gifts for friends who enjoy cooking.

◪ Shelves built on to the outside of this window frame make a well-lit, practical place for growing an array of different herbs. The double window ensures that although on the outside of the first wire screen, they are protected from frost by the external window.

◀ Rosemary, chervil , thyme, basil and parsley make an attractive display of contrasting leaf shapes and shades of green in this unusual wooden container. Tie a ribbon round a bunch of the herbs to hang on a door or a wall.

FLORAL AND HERB PLAIT

Displays of dried flowers, herbs and spices make practical alternatives to fresh floral arrangements.

A decorative roll of dried flowers, herbs and spices makes a delightful, semi-permanent fragrant display which will add cheer to any kitchen when hung on a wall. Though the plait is mainly decorative, it could have culinary uses, too, if you keep some bay leaves and other favourite herbs in the small terracotta pots ready to be added to your cooking.

Any combination of dried flowers, herbs, fruits and spices can be used, provided there is variety in shape and texture. Use readily available materials –

either bought dried flowers, seedheads and foliage, or fresh material you have dried yourself. If you like, you can introduce a seasonal harvest note to the finished plait with ears of wheat, barley and other dried grasses.

It's easier to work on a flat tabletop while making the plait, but remember that it will be hung up when finished. Make sure to wire heavier items tightly so that they don't droop, and hold it up every now and then to see how gravity affects your arrangement.

his floral and
rb plait adds a
untry touch to any
om in your home.
ang it in the kitchen
d you could use
e ingredients when
u cook.

MAKING A PLAIT

All the materials are wired on to a frame of chicken wire and moss. The technique is very straightforward, but to protect your hands, you may want to wear gloves. Stub wire and sphagnum moss are sold by florists and large garden centres. Look for chicken wire in DIY or garden centres.

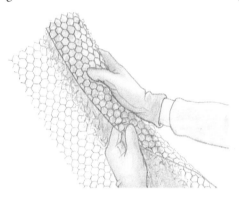
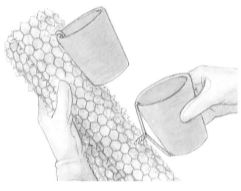

1 Making the wire frame Using wire cutters, cut a piece of chicken wire about 60cm (24in) long by 30cm (12in) wide. Arrange a tightly packed plait of dried sphagnum moss along the length. Wrap the wire around the moss, overlapping the long edges to form a cylinder. Twist the loose ends of the wire back into the mesh to secure the roll.

2 Wiring the pots Thread a 25cm (10in) length of stub wire through the drainage hole in the pot and twist the ends together into a single sturdy stem. Attach it near the top of the plait by pushing the wire stem right through the moss and mesh. Twist tightly round the chicken wire at the back to secure. Repeat for the other pots, attaching one in the centre and one at the base.

3 Wiring the pomegranates With a fine skewer make a hole through the base of a dried pomegranate. Thread a length of stub wire through the hole and twist the ends to form a stem. Push this through the wire framework just below the top pot and secure at the back. Repeat with the other pomegranates, arranging all three as a group.

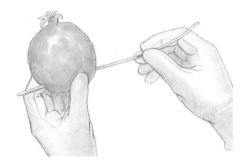

4 Wiring the hydrangea Twist one end of a piece of stub wire around a hydrangea stem. Push the other end of the wire through the framework at the top and anchor at the back. Repeat for the other hydrangea heads, positioning them in a zigzag down its length.

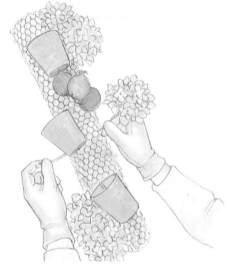

5 Filling in the plait Wire in the marjoram, chillies, apple rings, linseed, lavender and roses in the same way, making sure to cover the front and sides of the plait evenly. Make three raffia bow shapes and attach them to the plait with stub wire just below each terracotta pot.

6 Filling the pots Put sprigs of bay leaves in the lowest pot, poppy seedheads in the middle pot and rosemary in the top pot. To hang the plait, thread a loop of twisted raffia through the top of the frame.

Dried roses, linseed, bay leaves, lavender and a pomegranate are just some of the ingredients used to make the plait.

TABLE SCENE-SETTERS

Dainty flower posies and bouquets to decorate place settings add a lovely freshness to a table, whether you are entertaining friends or just treating yourself and your family.

Adding colour and freshness to a breakfast table, each eggcup posy has its own special charm, with a different emphasis of colour and shape in all four little cups. The flowers – single daisies, blue cornflowers, single yellow chrysanthemums – were picked for their simple forms and to match the table linen and china.

These colourful, fragrant table posies take next to no time to get together, need a minimum of expertise and no special equipment, and cost very little. A natural look of unaffected freshness is the key to success – unlike carefully arranged elaborate displays, mini-posies rely for their charm on a few flowers artlessly set in a container.

Whether you're picking flowers from the garden or buying from a florist, look for modest little flowers with simple shapes such as single daisies – try to avoid big showy double blooms. Flowers such as sweet peas and pinks are ideal, as they have a lovely sweet scent as well as an old-fashioned charm.

Choose colours to coordinate with your table linen and china, or with the colour scheme of the room in general. For containers, use the same, or similar, china as that laid on the table – dainty eggcups, a little jug, teacups or a teapot all work well for a table arrangement.

When you cut the stems to length, angle the cut to give as large a surface area as possible for plenty of water to be taken up. For a posy arrangement, turn the container as you add the flowers, to make sure the display looks good from all sides.

TABLE TREATS

Both of these displays are easy to arrange, using garden or florist's flowers that coordinate with the setting – even in deepest winter you can buy a few rose or carnation blooms. Check the level of water in the teapot and keep it topped up so the flowers stay fresh for as long as possible. Stand the little bouquets in water until they are needed – when the meal is over, guests can keep the flowers as a dainty memento of the evening, or the bouquets can be popped back in water so they keep fresh for a little longer.

▼ A posy in a teapot is particularly appropriate on a table set for tea. Flowers such as sweet peas, stocks and roses were chosen for their sweet scent as well as their delicate charm.

TEAPOT POSY

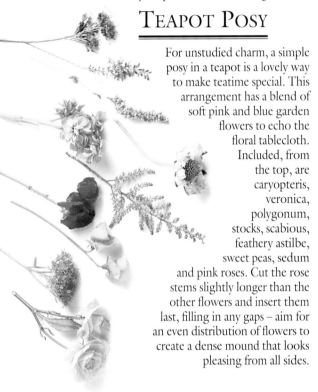

For unstudied charm, a simple posy in a teapot is a lovely way to make teatime special. This arrangement has a blend of soft pink and blue garden flowers to echo the floral tablecloth. Included, from the top, are caryopteris, veronica, polygonum, stocks, scabious, feathery astilbe, sweet peas, sedum and pink roses. Cut the rose stems slightly longer than the other flowers and insert them last, filling in any gaps – aim for an even distribution of flowers to create a dense mound that looks pleasing from all sides.

MINI-BOUQUET

Four types of flowers were used for this delicate little table cluster – blue cornflowers, shell pink chrysanthemums, pink plumed polygonum and a creamy yellow rose.

For each mini-bouquet, divide the flowers into little groups of roughly equal stem lengths, then gather the groups together into a cluster held in place with a twist of fine florist's wire. If necessary, trim the stem ends to neaten. For a final flourish and to hide the wire, tie florist's ribbon or lace around the stems.

▲ Individual bouquets grace a more formal table – present each of your guests with a miniature bouquet beside the place setting.

SPRING MEDLEY

Taking your cue from nature, arrange a display that brings a touch of spring into your home with flowering bulbs which have all the fresh charm of those growing naturally outdoors.

There's nothing more cheering than the sight of spring bulbs pushing their way through the hard earth and unfolding their flowers to announce winter is over. A bowl of flowering bulbs has long been a favourite indoor display – what's refreshing about the arrangements shown here and overleaf is that they borrow ideas from nature.

Just like bulbs left to naturalize in the wild, they are close planted and grouped informally, and each display has a grass or mossy underplanting. The arrangements couldn't be simpler to get together – as well as the ideas given overleaf, you can experiment with different spring effects, whether it be a host of golden daffodils or a cloud of purple crocuses.

What could be more magical than creating on your dining table a little corner of a mossy woodland dell or a spring meadow, complete with flowering bulbs?

An informal planting of bulbs brings spring to a table. For an instant display, buy ready-grown bulbs, set them in a large container and add a few tufts of grass.

SPRING DISPLAY

Buy three or four pots of ready-grown bulbs which are in bud. Avoid any with open blooms as they won't last long. For a fairly instant effect look for fat buds which will soon open in normal room temperatures.

You don't need to disturb the bulbs by transplanting them – simply set them in their original pots in a suitable container. A large, fairly shallow dish or bowl of about the same depth as the pots usually works well. You'll need to line a container like a wicker basket with polythene before adding the pots.

The easiest finishing touch for your spring display is to tuck a layer of moss – bun, sphagnum or reindeer are available from most florist's – over the top of the pots and around the bulb stems. Make sure you fill the spaces between the pots so that your arrangement looks like one planting.

Alternatively, create a realistic underplanting with grass or fresh moss from a garden. Firm a few handfuls of compost around the pots in the container, mounding it up if appropriate for as natural a look as possible. Either plant some tufts of grass lifted from a corner of a lawn, or add a layer of moss.

Fresh moss can often be found in the corner of a garden, or at the side of a path or foot of a wall. Ease up as large a mat of moss as you can, then tuck the mossy mats over the compost – the joins will soon grow over, and you can cover any bare patches with pebbles. Keep the mossy pad moist so that it remains fresh and green.

▲ *With their spicy scent, hyacinths are ideal as a spring centrepiece. For a natural effect the trick with bulbs is to group them informally and add a carpet of moss.*

▶ *The delicacy of these crocuses is enhanced by the pebble-strewn mossy mound. If you can't get fresh moss from a garden, use bun or reindeer moss, available from florist's, for ground cover.*

BULB POSITION

To keep your display looking good and avoid the forced, leggy look of bulbs kept indoors, aim for a setting as close to the outdoor conditions as possible.

A spot that is light but out of direct sunshine, and well away from draughts or heat source, is ideal. If possible, leave the bulbs in a cool place, such as a spare room, and move them into their display position when needed.

TRIMMED BASKETS

*Wicker baskets decorated with fresh greenery or delicate sprays
of dried flowers make perfect fruit holders, adding a touch of
style and colour to any tabletop.*

It's simple to transform a plain wicker basket into an eye-catching feature by trimming the edge with foliage or small bunches of dried flowers. Attaching the decorations couldn't be easier and you will be delighted at the natural effect achieved.

For a pleasing colour scheme, choose foliage or flowers that coordinate with the general style of your room or try to match the trim with the contents of the basket. Here, glossy ivy leaves are combined with shiny lemons and limes to create a fresh, summery look that blends well with the yellow and white striped tablecloth — notice how well the dark green of the ivy

enhances the fresh hues of the citrus fruit.

Ivy is particularly suitable for decorating wicker baskets, as it is easy to find and grows in long, flexible strands, perfect for threading through the basket weave. Alternatively you can buy artificial ivy and use it to create a longer-lasting display. For an ivy trim, bear in mind that the basket must have a fairly open weave so that the stems can be pushed through easily. Use thin fuse wire to attach the thickest part of the ivy stem to the basket in a few places around the edge.

A simple method of trimming a basket with dried flowers to make another pretty display is given overleaf.

Ivy makes a simple yet elegant trim for decorating a plain basket. Here, fresh variegated ivy has been used for a short-term display.

DRIED FLOWER TRIM

Practical as well as pretty, a dried flower decoration makes a long-lasting trim for a wicker basket, producing an attractive holder for fresh fruit, bread or even sweet-smelling soaps. The warm colour scheme used here ties in well with the rich hues of red and purple fruit, but you can vary the dried flowers as you like to create a different mood to suit the contents of the basket. To show off a dried flower trim best, choose a basket with a small rim and a central handle.

For the trim shown here that decorates just one side of the basket, the flowers are first wired into two small bunches. These are then placed stem to stem at the base of the handle

with the join hidden by extra flowers. Build up each bunch in your hand, wiring the stems together as you add flowers.

To make one bunch, take some lavender sprigs and arrange a head of nipplewort on either side. Wind wire round the stems to hold them. Position two roses at the front, a carthamus on each side with three eryngiums in the centre, and wind wire round the stems again. Trim the stems to about 5cm (2in). Repeat to make a second bunch, then place the bunches end to end with stems overlapping and wire them together. Wire the bunches to the basket at the base of the handle and wire three helichrysums over the join to hide it.

◄ *Examples of the dried flowers used in the spray include, from the top, carthamus, lavender, eryngium, nipplewort, roses and helichrysums.*

SIMPLE ALTERNATIVES

For a fragrant addition to a chintzy, cottage-style room, attach rows of small dried roses around the edge of a basket, then fill the basket with rose-scented pot pourri. A basket with a handle looks particularly attractive

❖

To add a touch of freshness to a guest room, attach a posy of dried herbs to the side of a shallow basket. Finish off the posy with a delicate ribbon and arrange soap and lotions in the basket.

❖

For an exotic display, try winding dried hops around the edge of a shallow basket and fill the basket with miniature dried gourds.

◄ *A perfect harmony of reds, pinks and purples, this flower trimmed basket, piled with luscious fresh fruit, makes a stunning display.*

CLASSIC TABLE CENTREPIECE

This clever table centrepiece is very simple and quick to put together, and is perfect for adding a decorative and sophisticated touch to a dining table set for a special occasion.

With its rich red roses, peach carnations, burnt orange alstroemeria and contrasting acid green euphorbia, this table centrepiece will add a decorative flourish to any dinner party or celebratory table setting.

Roses, alstroemeria and carnations are available all the year round, so you can recreate this arrangement in any season. If you have difficulty finding euphorbia, substitute it with a filler material, such as *Alchemilla mollis*, solidago or a green variety of small-flowered chrysanthemum. If you prefer, you can use your own choice of flowers

and greenery for the arrangement. When deciding on flowers and colours, consider what else is on the table. Let your choice be guided by the designs on the china and table linen, or by the overall scheme of the room – the colours and patterns on curtains and other furnishings or a strong wall colour are good starting points – or simply go for the prettiest flowers available.

The arrangement is made using a block of florists' foam as a base. Put the foam on to a flat plate to protect the table surface – the plate won't show once the flowers are in place.

This formal table arrangement will certainly give your guests something to talk about. The red roses catch the eye, as they nestle into a bed of euphorbia, carnations and alstroemeria.

MAKING THE CENTREPIECE

The centrepiece is designed to be seen from all sides, so space the flowers equally on the foam base. At the same time, make sure you keep the arrangement low, so it won't interfere with people's ability to see and talk to each other as they dine.

When sticking the foliage and flowers into the florists' foam, don't worry too much about spacing every stem correctly the first time. You can fiddle with the arrangement as you go, and once you have finished, to find the final look.

YOU WILL NEED

- ❖ FLORISTS' FOAM, 13cm (5in) square
- ❖ FLAT DINNER PLATE
- ❖ SCISSORS
- ❖ BUNCH OF LIME GREEN EUPHORBIA
- ❖ BUNCH OF PEACH SPRAY CARNATIONS
- ❖ THREE STEMS OF ORANGE ALSTROEMERIA
- ❖ SIX 'VICKI BROWN' RED ROSES
- ❖ FIVE STEMS OF GOLD VARIEGATED SMALL-LEAVED IVY

1 Preparing the foam Fill a plastic basin with cold water. Place the florists' foam on the water and leave it to absorb the water for 15 minutes or until the block has sunk to the bottom of the basin.

3 Fixing the euphorbia Stick the sprigs of euphorbia into the foam block, covering both the top and the sides evenly. Make sure all the sprigs are stuck in to the same depth, so they form a uniform 'hedgehog' shape. Keep back a few sprigs to add at the final stage.

5 Adding the alstroemeria Insert the stems of alstroemeria between the carnations, being careful to maintain the domed shape of the arrangement. Check the shape by slowly turning the arrangement, adjusting the ingredients as necessary.

From top to bottom, the ingredients for this classic table centrepiece are euphorbia, alstroemeria, carnations, roses and ivy.

2 Preparing the flowers Split the euphorbia into small pieces with stems of equal length. Trim the alstroemeria and carnation stems down to about 7.5cm (3in) long.

4 Adding the carnations Holding the carnations just below the head so they don't break, stick the stems into the foam, distributing them evenly in the foliage.

6 Adding the roses Insert one rose at the top of the arrangement and space the remaining five roses in among the other ingredients, experimenting for the best effect.

7 Finishing the arrangement If you notice any gaps, add the remaining sprigs of euphorbia. Tuck a few pieces of ivy into the lower part of the arrangement to add a little more interest and to ensure that the plate is completely concealed.

The traditional appeal of this compact dresser is emphasized by a collection of country-style blue and white china. The quaint china duck and jug of dried blooms set a central focal point for the balanced display.

SMARTLY DRESSED

Proudly displaying best china, favourite ornaments and memorabilia, a dresser becomes a focal point in a dining room or kitchen. It also provides valuable extra storage.

From a small, humble dresser that fits snugly into an out-of-the-way corner, to the most grandiose piece, dressers always draw the eye. Decorative in their own right, once they are set with china or treasured ornaments, they take on a unique charm that reflects the personality of those that live in the home.

The starting point is the dresser itself. Traditionally in natural, varnished timber, dressers are now also stained or painted to match the theme of a room. There is no need to be timid with the choice of colour if you decide to paint a dresser – bright blue, sea green or sunshine yellow can all be a distinctive backdrop for

your display. The ornaments can compete with their setting – try bold yellow crockery on a deep green dresser for modern impact; or the dresser can provide a foil – what better way to show off white plates than on a vivid blue shelf?

Use the dresser to display china in everyday use – it's easy to reach and see. Alternatively, choose pieces just for display and keep your working china neatly stored away in the cupboard below. While the shelves of the dresser are perfect for plates and cups, the dresser top makes an ideal home for larger bowls and plates, storage jars and jugs and even a vase of fresh flowers.

◀ *Rich buttermilk cream is the mellow choice for this dresser. The style of the dresser is pure country, yet the choice of a cream paint finish gives it a dressier feel, more suited to a dining room setting. Pretty plates with red flowery motifs are perfectly at home on the shelves and introduce some welcome pattern into the understated room scheme.*

◣ *Colour-rubbed pine, painted in a vibrant turquoise, is the perfect setting for a collection of wicker-wrapped carafes and jugs, and earthenware in luminous yellow. The dresser top, left in rich natural pine, ensures the total effect has warmth.*

▲ *For a twist on the blue and white theme, this dresser is painted electric blue and set with plain white china. The intense blue is achieved by painting over a base coat of copper red. Wire-fronted cupboard doors become the focus, rather than the items on display, yet the bold white plates still show through.*

PAINTING CHINA

*Plain crockery becomes a colourful, decorative accessory when
it's hand-painted in a bright, imaginative way. A few deft brush strokes in
special ceramic paint is all that it takes.*

Y‌ou can paint any type of plain, glazed
or unglazed crockery or china. To
begin with use inexpensive pieces
that are not too large – plates and
saucers are ideal for first attempts. Painting is also a good way of cheering up an
old chipped piece such as a vase or
teapot that you can't use any more.

If you are buying new china, white is
the best choice, as coloured crockery
alters the colour of the paint. The other
advantage of using white is that it is
readily available – the cheaper kitchen
ranges usually offer a wide range of suitable items. Alternatively, you can use

plain white china blanks – plates, jars
and dishes which are specially produced
for decorating and available from craft
shops.

It is important to remember that you
can only use your hand-painted china
for decorative purposes as some ceramic
paints may be toxic. Also, as the china is
not refired after it has been painted, it
will not withstand the repeated washing
that items like plates and teacups
require. You can wash this hand-painted
china gently in lukewarm water with a
little mild detergent, but it should not
be put in a dishwasher.

*Hand-painted china is meant
to be shown off – on a dresser,
the top of a cabinet or
mounted directly on a wall.
Simple geometric and abstract
patterns like these are easy to
paint, and make a colourful
splash when several pieces are
displayed together.*

PAINTING ON CHINA

Special paints for use on ceramics are stocked by craft and art shops, and are available by mail order. This china was painted with a solvent-based ceramic paint that does not require firing or varnishing. Some paints, however, do need to be varnished for protection – check this when buying the paints.

Geometric patterns and freehand floral motifs are an easy starting point. For clear geometric patterns, use a masking off technique – the dot, heart and diamond patterns shown on the opening page were all formed in this way. For freehand designs, you can paint directly on to the plate – you may like to practise your pattern on paper first.

When painting the china, it's important to let one colour dry before applying the next, as wet colours will run into each other.

1 Preparing to paint Remove all traces of dust or grease by wiping over the china with a soft cloth, dipped in methylated spirits (denatured alcohol). Leave the surface to dry before starting to apply the paint.

A simple design produces effective results, as this bright and cheerful painted plate demonstrates.

2 Painting the petals Use a size 6 brush and blue paint for the flowers. Working from the centre out, paint each petal in a single stroke. With the corner of a cloth, rub off the paint in each flower centre. Leave the paint to dry.

3 Filling in the background Using a size 10 brush and yellow paint, fill in the background colour and the centre of the flowers. Don't worry if you paint over some of the petals, as you will repaint these later on to neaten them. Again leave the paint to dry thoroughly.

4 Neatening the design Using the size 6 brush and blue, repaint the petals, leaving the yellow centres of the flowers showing. Allow the paint to dry. Clean the brush thoroughly with white spirit.

5 Adding leaves On an old saucer, mix blue and yellow paint to get green. Using a size 6 brush, paint single strokes of green in the shape of a comma over the background to resemble leaves. Leave the paint to dry. If required, varnish.

MASKING METHOD

To mask off areas to form a geometric design, you can use masking tape or self-adhesive labels. First prepare the china by wiping it with methylated spirits (denatured alcohol), then press the masking tape or self-adhesive labels firmly down on the surface. Use circles for a dotty design, strips of tape for stripes, or cut out simple shapes, such as hearts.

Apply the paint over the surface, leave it to dry, then peel off the tape or labels to reveal the unpainted china. You can leave the resulting motifs unpainted or paint them in a different colour.

Painting a diamond pattern Stick parallel strips of masking tape across the surface so they almost touch. Apply more strips diagonally across the first ones. Using a craft knife, cut round alternate diamonds of tape and peel them off. Using a round artists' brush, paint the exposed diamond shapes. Leave the paint to dry before removing the tape. If necessary, apply varnish.

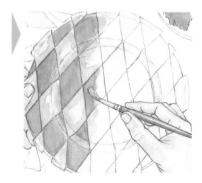

WIRE-FRONTED CUPBOARDS

Add character and interest to a plain wooden cupboard by replacing the door panel with wire mesh. It's a highly adaptable look – equally suited to an informal country kitchen or a modern living room.

W ire-fronted cupboards are popular, decorative items of furniture. Traditionally a country look associated with French farmhouses, antique examples of wire-fronted cupboards carry a price tag to match their desirability. In lovely aged timbers, or faded, mellow paintwork, these authentic examples are very rustic in look and include all sorts from small 'foodsafe' cupboards through to large dressers.

If you like the look of wire-fronted cupboards, you can try recreating the effect yourself. It's fairly easy to refit both new and old cupboards with a wire panel, provided they have an existing panel of glass or timber. It's a look that is particularly appropriate for rejuvenating an old cupboard – a car-boot or garage sale or junk shop find perhaps.

Although originally found in a kitchen, where the wire mesh keeps fresh produce ventilated, these rustic treasures can add a novel touch to other rooms. In a bedroom, with colourful clothes folded inside, they make an unusual bedside table, while in a study they are a unexpected alternative to a glass-fronted bookcase. You can either leave the wire mesh open or, for a softer, prettier look, you could back it with a fabric curtain.

A large, reclaimed linen cupboard, painted in bold blue and fitted with wire panels, finds a new home in a study. This is an example of a door with a rebate – the wire sits in the rebate and is held in place by wooden beading. The wire doors allow the contents of the cupboard, including some jazzy files covered in animal print fabrics, to be on display.

PREPARING A CUPBOARD

Hunt for an old cupboard in a salvage or second-hand shop or at a car boot or garage sale. Or you may already have an old cupboard that is begging for a facelift. Suitable candidates should have panels of glass or timber that you can easily knock out.

To make the job easy, it's important to find a cupboard where the existing panel is simply pinned to the back of the door or fitted into a rebate (recess) in the front or back of the door and the edge covered with hardwood beading. Avoid glass or wooden panels that are fitted into the frame itself, as they are tricky to remove and it is usually too difficult to fix the wire into the slot left by the glass or wood.

CHOOSING MATERIALS

You can buy all the materials you need from a hardware store. All of the examples shown here use standard chicken wire. For a wire-fronted cupboard, buy a roll of the smallest width – 600mm (2ft) – and the finest mesh size – 13mm (½in) – available. Garden wire, which is more rigid, with a square rather than a hexagonal grid, also works well. To find out how much wire and lath or beading you need, remove the panel from the door and measure the opening left by the panel, including the rebate where appropriate.

REPAIRING THE CUPBOARD

Before you start fitting the wire into the door frame, examine the cupboard carefully to see if you need to treat it for woodworm and make any repairs necessary to the woodwork and joints to ensure that it is sturdy. Then concentrate on cleaning the cupboard up, removing the existing fittings and getting it ready to paint or varnish, following the instructions on the right. If or when it is in good condition, remove the door, then proceed with the appropriate instructions for removing the panel and fitting the wire.

1 Cleaning up the cupboard Check the cupboard for any signs of woodworm and treat it with a proprietary woodworm fluid before bringing it indoors. Stand the cupboard on newspaper and give it a good wipe down inside and out.

2 Removing the existing fittings Remove any door fittings. Unscrew the hinges and lift off the door. Check how the panel is fitted and follow the instructions (opposite or overleaf) to remove that type of panel.

3 Preparing to paint If the paint or varnish is in a bad state, use a chemical stripper to remove it. Apply primer before repainting. If the paint or varnish is sound, rub over it with a piece of fine sandpaper to remove any uneven areas and to key the surface, ready for painting.

FITTING WIRE TO A REBATED DOOR

This method shows how to fit wire to a door which has a rebate. The edges of the wire end up hidden under hardwood beading, which sits down in the rebate. Before you start, clean and prepare the cupboard. If you can prise the old beading out without damaging it, you can re-fit it using new nails – after all, it matches and fits the cupboard. If you buy new hardwood beading, choose a size and shape to match the wood of the door and the depth of the rebate.

These instructions apply to panels that are fitted to either the back or the front of a door. If you are attaching the wire to the front, use a nail punch to hammer the nails below the surface and apply filler to conceal them before painting or varnishing the door.

1 Removing the panel If the existing wood or glass panel is held in place with beading, use a chisel, flat edge down, to prise it off. Prise off a long piece of beading first. Use pincers or pliers to remove the nails or cut through them if you can't pull them out. Once the first long piece is out, the two shorter pieces and the other long piece follow in turn. Push out the panel or use a hammer to tap it out lightly, keeping it intact if possible.

2 Cutting the wire Lay the chicken wire out flat and put the old door panel on top. Mark round the edge and then use wire cutters to cut out the wire. Put the door frame down flat, with the rebate upward. Straighten out the wire and fit it squarely into the rebate.

3 Cutting the beading Use the panel opening in the door to mark the cutting lines on the beading. Then use a tenon saw and a mitre box to cut four pieces with 45° ends – two to the length of the panel opening and two to its width. Check the beading fits neatly and trim the ends if necessary.

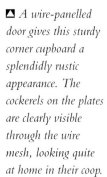

◄ A wire-panelled door gives this sturdy corner cupboard a splendidly rustic appearance. The cockerels on the plates are clearly visible through the wire mesh, looking quite at home in their coop.

◄ A close-up of the inside of the cupboard door shows how the strips of beading hold the wire tightly into the rebate of the door.

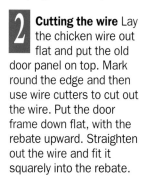

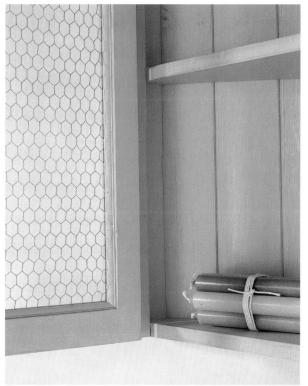

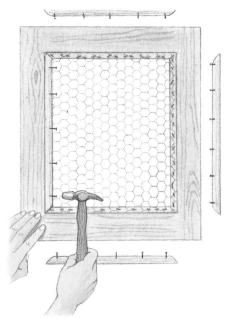

4 Fitting the wire Place the chicken wire squarely in the rebate and, using panel pins, nail one piece of beading to the side of the rebate – it helps if you knock the panel pins part of the way into the beading first. Then use pliers to pull the wire taut and fit the beading on the opposite side of the panel opening. Fit the two other pieces of beading in the same way. If you find it hard to cope with the wire, staple it in place first.

5 Replacing the door On a door front, knock in the pin heads with a nail punch and fill with wood filler. Rehang the door, asking a friend to hold it as you refit the hinges; replace any handles. Paint the cupboard as desired.

FITTING A WIRE PANEL FROM THE BACK

With this method, you attach the wire to the flat back of the door frame and hide the rough edges of the wire under lengths of lath. Prepare the cupboard in the same way as for *Fitting Wire to a Rebated Door*.

YOU WILL NEED

- ❖ PLAIN WOODEN PANELLED CUPBOARD
- ❖ SCREWDRIVER
- ❖ PINCERS
- ❖ HAMMER
- ❖ 13mm (½in) GAUGE CHICKEN WIRE
- ❖ PLIERS OR WIRE CUTTERS
- ❖ HARDWOOD (RAMIN) LATH 25 x 6mm (1 x ¼in)
- ❖ TENON SAW
- ❖ 19mm (¾in) PANEL PINS

1 Dismantling the cupboard front
Use pincers to remove the panel pins which hold the door panel in position. Working from the outside of the door push out the panel.

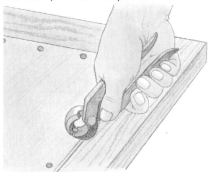

2 Cutting the wire mesh Using the original door panel as a template, with a pair of pliers or wire cutters cut out a sheet of chicken wire 13mm (½in) larger all round.

3 Cutting the lath Cut two lengths of lath equal to the width (**A**) of the door panel opening. Cut two more lengths equal to the height (**B**) of the opening plus twice the width of the lath (**C**). Check that once you've fitted the lath the door is still going to close properly against any shelves inside.

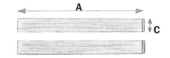

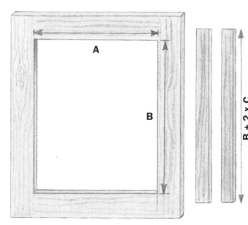

▲ *As the contents are easy to see through the chicken wire, each item is picked to match the colour of the cupboard itself. The back of the cupboard door has no rebate, so the wire is held in place with strips of lath.*

4 Fixing the wire with laths
Straighten out the chicken wire so that it sits squarely behind the empty panel. Lay the laths over the edges of the wire and fix in position with panel pins. Hammer the pins in at a slight angle through the centre of the lath. (If you put them too close to the edge it may split.) Refit the door and paint as desired.

126

Index

ACKNOWLEDGEMENTS

Photographs

7 EWA/Rodney Hyett, 8(t) Ikea, 8(b) EWA/Andreas von Einsiedel, 9(t) EWA/Tommy Candler, 9(b) EWA/Tom Leighton, 10(t) EWA/Michael Dunne, 10(b) Magnet, 11 EWA, 12-13(tl) Ariadne Holland, 12-13(b) EWA/Clive Helm, 13(tr,br) EWA/Michael Dunne, 14(t) EWA/Tim Street-Porter, 14(bl) EWA/Rodney Hyett, 14(br) Zeyko, 15, 16(bl) WorldWide Syndication, 16(br) Lakeland Plastics, 16-17(tc) IPC Magazines/Robert Harding Syndication, 17(tr) Cotteswood, 17(b) Graham Kitchens, 18(tl,tr) Lakeland Plastics, 18(bl,br) WorldWide Syndication, 19 Magnet, 20-21(l) CP Hart, 20(bl), 21(tr) Eaglemoss Publications/Simon Page-Ritchie, 21(br) WorldWide Syndication, 22(tl) Eaglemoss Publications/Simon Page-Ritchie, 22(tr) IPC Magazines/Robert Harding Syndication, 22(bl) Crabtree Kitchens, 23(tl) Eaglemoss Publications/Simon Page-Ritchie, 23(tr) Fired Earth, 22-23(bl) IPC Magazines/Robert Harding Syndication, 24(t) EWA/Rodney Hyett, 24(b) CP Hart, 24-25(tl) Eaglemoss Publications/Simon Page-Ritchie, 26-27(tl) Hygena at MFI, 26-27(bl) Whitton Wood Designs, 26-27(br), 27(tr) Ikea, 27(br) Wrighton Kitchens, 28(t) Hygena at MFI, 28(bl) Wrighton Kitchens, 28-29(bl) Alno, 29(tl) Miele, 29(tr,br) Ikea, 30(t) Hayloft Woodwork, 30(bl) Zeyko, 30(br) Schreiber Kitchens at MFI, 31 IPC Magazines/Robert Harding Syndication, 32-33(tl) Astracast Plc, 32(b) Whitehall Fabrications, 33(tr) Astracast Plc, 33(b) EWA/Jon Bouchier, 34(bl) CP Hart, 34-35(t) WorldWide Syndication, 34-35(bc) EWA/Rodney Hyett, 35(br) Elon Ltd, 36(t) Blanco, 36(bl) Ariadne Holland, 36(br) Magnet, 37 David Parmiter, 38(cl) EWA/Rodney Hyett, 38-39(b) Magnet, 39(t) EWA/Andreas von Einsiedel, 40(t) EWA/Friedhelm Thomas, 40(b) WorldWide Syndication, 41(t) EWA/Peter Woloszynski, 41(b) EWA/Andreas von Einsiedel, 42(t) EWA/Brian Harrison, 42(bl) Siematic, 42(br) EWA/Tom Leighton, 43 IPC Magazines/Robert Harding Syndication, 44-45(tl) Robert Harding Picture Library, 44-45(bl) WorldWide Syndication, 45(tr), 45(br) IPC Magazines/Robert Harding Syndication, 46(t) Ikea, 46(b) Robert Harding Picture Library, 47 WorldWide Syndication, 48(l) EWA/Neil Lorimer, 48-49(t) EWA/Tim Street-Porter, 48-49(b) IPC Magazines/Robert Harding Syndication, 49(r) WorldWide Syndication, 50(t) EWA/Nadia McKenzie, 50(b) Zanussi, 51 Schreiber Kitchens at MFI, 52-53(t) Wickes, 52(b), 54-55(tl,bl) Hygena at MFI, 55(tr,c) Wickes, 56(t) MFI, 56(c) Wickes, 56(bl) Magnet, 56(br) Texas Homecare, 57 Ikea, 58(b) EWA/David Giles, 58-59(t) WorldWide Syndication, 59(bl) EWA/Tommy Candler, 60 IPC Magazines/Robert Harding Syndication, 61 Magnet, 62, 63(tl) MFI, 63(tr) Alno, 63(b) Keller Kitchens, 64(l) WorldWide Syndication, 64(tr) Ariston, 64(b) Magnet, 65 Zeyko, 66-67(t) Ikea, 67(br) Chippendale Kitchens, 68(l,br) Mobalpa Cuisines, 68(cr) WorldWide Syndication, 69(br) Texas Homecare, 69(tl) WorldWide Syndication, 69(cr) Ikea, 69(br) Wrighton Kitchens/Texas Homecare, 70(t) WorldWide Syndication, 70(bl) Mobalpa Cuisines, 70(br) Ikea, 71, 72-73 IPC Magazines/Robert Harding Syndication, 73(b) Magnet, 74(t) EWA/Michael Dunne, 74(bl) EWA/Spike Powell, 74(br) EWA/Andreas von Einsiedel, 75 EWA/Spike Powell, 76-77 IPC Magazines/Robert Harding Syndication, 78(tr) EWA/Tom Leighton, 78(b) IPC Magazines/Robert Harding Syndication, 79(t) Chippendale Kitchens, 79(b) IPC Magazines/Robert Harding Syndication, 80(tr) Ariadne Holland, 80(cl) EWA/Spike Powell, 80(bl,br) IPC Magazines/Robert Harding Syndication, 81 Andrew Macintosh Kitchens, 82-83 Smallbone Kitchens, 84(b) IPC Magazines/Robert Harding Syndication, 84-85(t) EWA/Michael Dunne, 85(bl) Lars Hallen/Design Press, 85(br) Rodney Hyett, 86(t) Eaglemoss Publications/Graham Rae, 86(cl) Eaglemoss Publications/Simon Page-Ritchie, 86(cr) Eaglemoss Publications/John Suett, 86(bl) Smallbone Kitchens, 86(br) Eaglemoss Publications/Simon Page Ritchie, 87 Ikea, 88-89 WorldWide Syndication, 90(t) EWA/Spike Powell, 90(bl) EWA/Rodney Hyett, 90(br) Magnet, 91 WorldWide Syndication, 92(t) IPC Magazines/Robert Harding Syndication, 92(cl) Divertimenti, 92(c) IPC Magazines/Robert Harding Syndication, 92(cr) Divertimenti, 92(b) Dulux, 93 Ariadne Holland, 94-95 IPC Magazines/Robert Harding Syndication, 96(t) DoehetZelf Holland, 96(bl,br) Ariadne Holland, 97(t) Abode UK, 97(b) B&Q, 98(t) EWA/Debi Treloar, 98(cl) Ariadne Holland, 98(bl) Eaglemoss Publications/Simon Page-Ritchie, 98(br) IPC Magazines/Robert Harding Syndication, 99, 100-101 IPC Magazines/Robert Harding Syndication, 102(tr) Ikea, 102(bl) Aktuell/Alternative Plans, 103(tr,bl) EWA/Rodney Hyett, 103(br) Eaglemoss Publications/Graham Rae, 104(tl) Boffi/Alternative Plans, 104(cl) Ikea, 104(cr,bl), 105, 106(tl,tr,c,bl) IPC Magazines/Robert Harding Syndication, 106(br) EWA/Ann Kelley, 107 WorldWide Syndication, 108(t) EWA/ Neil Lorimer, 108(cl,cr) WorldWide Syndication, 108(bl) Eaglemoss Publications/Martin Chaffer, 108(br) IPC Magazines/Robert Harding Syndication, 109 Eaglemoss Publications/Simon Page-Ritchie, 110 Eaglemoss Publications/Steve Tanner, 111-112 Eaglemoss Publications/Simon Page-Ritchie, 113 Marie Claire IdÇes/Maltaverne/Faver, 114 EWA/Di Lewis, 115(t) Eaglemoss Publications/Sue Atkinson, 115(br) Sue Atkinson, 115(br) Eaglemoss Publications/John Suett, 116 Eaglemoss Publications/Sue Atkinson, 117-118 Eaglemoss Publications/Simon Page-Ritchie, 119 Alvey & Towers, 120(t) EWA/Anaya, 120(bl,br) IPC Magazines/Robert Harding Syndication, 121 IPC Magazines/Robert Harding Syndication, 122 Eaglemoss Publications/Simon Page-Ritchie, 123 IPC Magazines/Robert Harding Syndication, 124-125 Eaglemoss Publications/Graham Rae, 126 Gentle & Boon.

Illustrations

52 James Culver, 53, 66 David Ashby, 110 Coral Mula, 122 Sally Holmes, 125-126 Coral Mula.